The Bellarmine Forum

OPTIMUS MMXXIII

The Best of 2013

The Wanderer Forum Foundation, Inc.
PO Box 542, Hudson, WI 54016-0542

ISBN: 978-0-991-5883-4-3
Photo Credits Listed in Back Matter

Editors: John B. Manos, John M. DeJak, and Cindy Paslawski

Layout: John B. Manos for the Bellarmine Forum

The Bellarmine Forum is a section 501(c)3 non-profit organization. Your tax deductible donation makes this and many other projects possible!

Etiam vel ho...
Hoc dixi?

The Two F...
wha

MARK, 10

...at many said, "He is...
...esus took him by the...
...him and he stood u...
...And when he had con...
...his disciples asked...
...8. "Why could not w...
...8. And he said to the...
...n be cast out in no...
prayer and fasting."
...cond Prediction of the P...
...d leaving that place,...

1965
MISSION STATEMENT

To: ~~The Wanderer Forum Foundation, Inc.~~
The Bellarmine Forum

YOUR MARCHING ORDERS:

The Bellarmine Forum is a network of lay Catholics who have banded together to promote and defend the true teachings of the Catholic Faith.

Our purpose is

* to educate and strengthen in faith all Catholics and their families

* - inform them on current issues relating to the Church's teachings;

* to support and defend the teaching authority of the Pope, the Vicar of Christ on earth; and,

* to encourage others to observe and uphold their Catholic Faith.

CONTENTS

EXORCISING THE VATICAN?

POPE FRANCIS STYLE

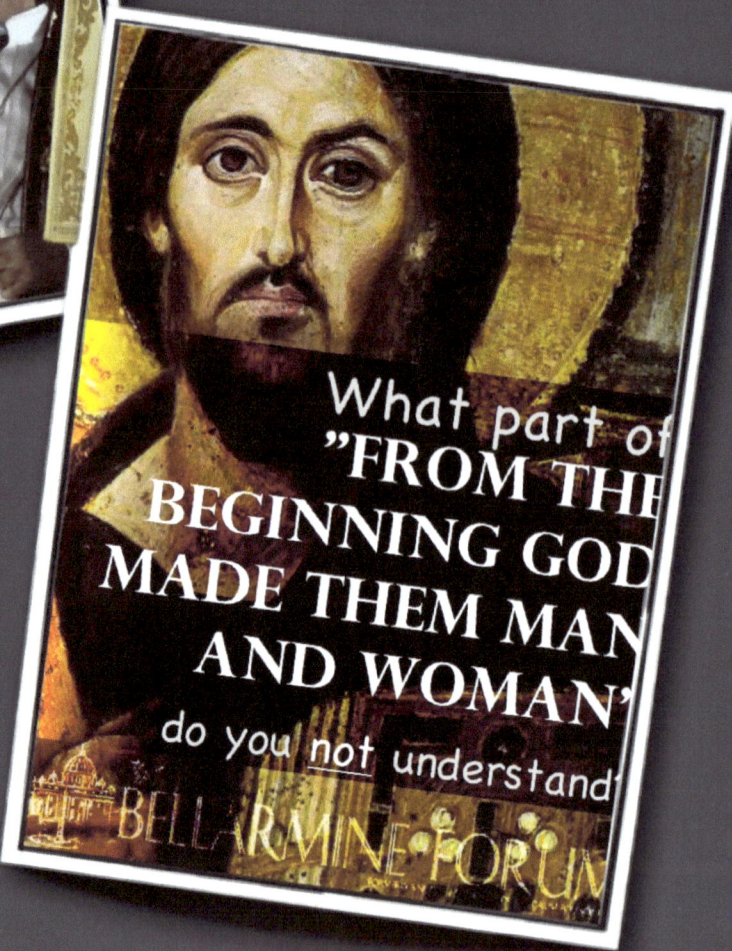

THE BELLARMINE FORUM

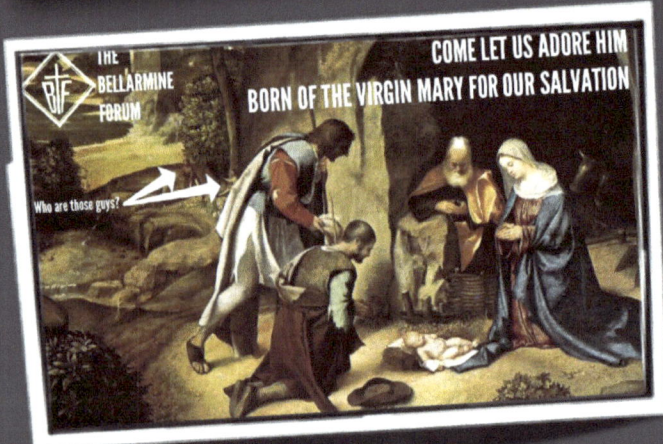

COME LET US ADORE HIM
BORN OF THE VIRGIN MARY FOR OUR SALVATION

Who are those guys?

What part of "FROM THE BEGINNING GOD MADE THEM MAN AND WOMAN" do you not understand?

BELLARMINE FORUM

WE'VE BEEN ON TOP OF ISSUES IN THE CHURCH FOR ALMOST 50 YEARS!

Forum Focus
A PUBLICATION OF THE WANDERER FORUM FOUNDATION

The Wanderer Forum Foundation, Inc.
P.O. Box 542, Hudson, WI 54016-0542

2003 Update...
The Catholic Campaign for Human Development

Forum Focus
A PUBLICATION OF THE WANDERER FORUM FOUNDATION

Vol. XVI, No. 4
Fall 2003

The Wanderer Forum Foundation, Inc.
P.O. Box 542, Hudson, WI 54016-0542

"Mary, the Mother of Life"
by Bishop Thomas Doran

Also Inside

"Mary, Mother and Mediatrix"
by Fr. Kenneth Baker, SJ

The BELLARMINE FORUM

Foreword

Dear Friends,

You are holding the "Best" of two worlds in your hands -- a print piece of cyberspace. By now you know, either as a subscriber to the *Bellarmine Forum* magazine or as a follower of the Bellarmine Forum website, that we present an ever-faithful yet unique, thought-provoking take on matters concerning the Church.

While the magazine presents a studious approach to our topics (Social Teachings in 2012, Vatican II in 2013, and the Right to Life in 2014), the website holds out the gut response to the news of the day, whether about the election of a new Pope or a government education plan that stinks.

The *Best of the Bellarmine Forum* is the ultimate crossover between both venues. These articles in *Best* were selected based on high readership. Several authors have written for our magazine. Some topics in these pages seem quirky -- "Baseball Cards Without Bubble Gum," and "My Last Ten Burials/Funerals With 'Fr. Strangelove,'" yet both point out profound truths on the abortion mentality. Others are short and to the point, like Arthur Hippler's "Confusions about Social Justice."

All are worth the read;, after all, it is truly the *Best* of the Bellarmine Forum and those associated with it.

My last ten burials/funerals with "Fr. Strangelove"… …or How I stop worrying and learned to love the (Demographic) Bomb, NOT!

by Fr. Timothy Sauppé

A stranger came into the sacristy after Sunday Mass. In an incriminating huff he said, "I have been away from the area for fifteen years; where are the people? And now you are tearing down the school? I went there as a kid." I put my hands up to quiet him from further talking and I calmly said, "Let me ask you a question: How many kids did you have?" He said, "Two." Then I said, "So did everyone else. When you only have two kids per family there is no growth." His demeanor changed, and then he dropped his head and said, "And they aren't even going to Mass anymore."

I never thought I would be asking that question, but since I had to close our parish school, I've grown bolder and I started to ask that question more often. When I came to my parish five years ago, the school was on its proverbial "last legs." In its last two years we did everything we could to recruit more students, but eventually I had to face the fact that after 103 years of education the school was no longer viable. In one of the pre-closure brainstorming sessions with teachers, I was asked what to do to get more students. I replied, "Well, I know what to do, but it takes seven years." The older teachers laughed, but the others needed me to state the obvious to the oblivious, *viz.* we need more babies. In my January 2010 letter to my bishop asking his permission to close our school, I wrote:

Bishop, it is with a heavy heart that I request this of you. As you know, priests were not ordained to be closing grade schools, but we were ordained to be Christ in the midst of sorrow and pain, which will be happening as we come to accept both your decision and the inevitable fact that St. Mary's Grade School is no longer viable. The efficient cause is simple….no children. The first cause is the habitual contraception and sterilization mentality of a good portion of married Catholic Christians–in short the Culture of Death. The final cause is the closure of Catholic Schools and parishes. Bishop, we need your leadership to address the contraception/abortion/sterilization mentality in as forceful a way as soon as possible.

I, and St. Mary's, closed the school that May 2010. Now three years later, I am razing the school building. It breaks my heart every time I go into this closed school. It is only 50 years old and yes, the windows and heating are in need of replacement, but otherwise the building is in good shape. You could not build as solid a building these days. There has not been a week without someone bringing the school closure and now razing up to me and how sad it is. But the cost of insurance and the cost of heating an empty building has become too burdensome for an aging and a decreasing congregation. A part of this decrease has happened because I have preached against the Culture of Death. I have modestly preached against contraception and sterilization, but for many of my parishioners it is too late. Most of them are done with raising more children. They have had their two kids twenty, thirty, forty years ago and some women don't want to hear about the Culture of Death. They decide to go to other parishes where the pastor doesn't prick their consciences. I am reminded of a diocesan official in his talk to us young pro-life, pro-family priests twenty years ago. He said, "Yes, you can preach against abortion and contraception, but remember, you have to put a roof over your churches." Now, our diocese is closing and merging these same parishes, but you know what—they all have good roofs.

Pastors, if the demographic winter or bomb seems someone else's problem, try this at your parish as I recently did at mine. I took the last ten burials and printed out their obituaries. At Sts. Peter and Paul Cemetery we had six men and four women with an average age of 80 years. With the ten, I counted the number of siblings for a total of 45 and divided by 10 which came to 4.5 children per family. Then I counted the ten's children and divided by ten. The next generation had 28 kids which I divided by ten and came to 2.8 per family. I then moved on to the third generation, the grandchildren. These ten deceased had 48 grandchildren from their 28 children. When dividing these numbers, I came to a figure of 1.714 per family. The national average number of children per household is 1.91[1]; while the replacement level is 2.1 children per family.

A recent internet story from a demographer from the University of New Hampshire reports that new census numbers show that one out of every three counties is losing population. My diocese did a demographic study for our Catholic school system, and they reported that our county will be losing ten percent each year to 2020; it is on the poverty watch list for Illinois. While the general economy is depressed and our local economy is very depressed, we cannot blame these demographic shifts simply on a lack of business. Of course, most pastors don't need the U.S. Census, we can see this decrease happening in our respective parishes from year to year. And of course, this is not just a Catholic phenomenon, it's across the cultural spectrum. To be blunt, there is a current bumper-sticker that encapsulates our era; and it ties in to our school closure. A veterinarian has just bought our fuel burners from our school boilers because he is expanding his business to include pet cremation. Why? For pet burials. And the current bumper sticker? "We love our granddogs!"

I don't claim to have answers on how to turn around a dying parish or diocese. In fact, I am more at a loss as to what to say than ever before. To defend the Church's teaching against contraception and sterilization is like going back to ancient Rome and warning them about the dangers of indoor lead plumbing. No matter what you would say their only response back would come in various levels of volume, "But it's indoor plumbing!" In other words, no matter the real threat to one's physical health from contraception and sterilization, the immediate perceived benefits outweigh the moral and physical downside. And, if there is contraceptive failure, i.e., a baby, women must have access to abortion; and if a couple is infertile, they can always create babies — in vitro. Further, the U.S. Food and Drug Administration has now allowed an over the counter, non-prescription abortifacient drug, "Plan B," to be given to those fifteen and older. Something as unique as one's gender, maleness or femaleness, is now being treated as a flexible concept. In short, the freedom or liberty to kill the unborn or the elderly; to contracept or to sterilize one's fertility; to have completely open and unrestricted sexual relationships are protected under the law because, "At the heart of liberty is the right to define one's concept of existence, of the universe, and of the mystery of human life" (Planned Parenthood v. Casey, 1992).

Having grown up in the 60's and 70's with many "Don't call me Father" priests, I knew that the problem was a lack of orthodoxy. Twenty years ago when I was ordained, I thought that if I just preached the faith and celebrated a solemn Sunday Mass people would turn around. But, after twenty

---

[1] cf. http://www.census.gov/hhes/families/files/cps2012/tabAVG3.xls - *ed. note: the link given is a table of statistics on households and family sizes broken down by education, race, or other statistics, showing that almost all groups are well below 2.1 children per household)*

Sometimes I feel like the Slim Pickens character from the 1964 movie, Dr. Strangelove, where he is riding the falling nuclear bomb; he, waving a cowboy hat; me, waving a biretta.

years, my experience is that a few parishioners will write letters to the Bishop, some will leave murmuring, but the standard fare is benign indifference. Instead of encountering joy and submission to the Natural Law and the Church's teaching on human life and its dignity, I have found Catholic Christians either complacent or complicit with the Culture of Death. It was reported that over fifty percent of Catholics voted for a pro-abortion president who at a recent Texas Planned Parenthood convention asked God to bless them. If I have found any fruit, it has mostly come from home-schooling families.

I have become convinced that there is a connection, a direct correlation, between contracepting or sterilizing one's fertility that parleys into an infertile relationship with Jesus, the Divine Bridegroom. In other words, mortal sin is the ultimate barrier method when it comes to God's gift of grace being implanted within our souls. It is known that Jesus expects us to be faithful in small things before He will entrust us with larger issues. What is smaller and yet has the greatest value than bringing new life into the world? The realpolitik, the *sitz im leben*, the situation on the ground, is that reproductive dissent has reached and surpassed a critical mass. Whether we are talking within or outside the church, tacit support is given to the culture of death when we don't support the Natural Law against all unnatural sexual actions. To wit, the arrogant aggrandizement of the state and Federal government under Obamacare and the HHS mandate over Catholic hospitals and educational institutions. Where will it end? (Cardinal George of Chicago has predicted that there may be no Catholics hospitals or colleges within two years.).

Sometimes I feel like the Slim Pickens character from the 1964 movie, *Dr. Strangelove*, where he is riding the falling nuclear bomb; he, waving a cowboy hat; me waving a biretta. (If not a biretta, perhaps a sixty degree sand-wedge.) What I should be doing instead is to try to defuse the demographic bomb; but the thing is, "God always forgives, man sometimes forgives, but nature....nature never forgives!" If the vast majority of Catholics chose to contracept

and sterilize themselves into the dust bin of history, what can God do? Of course, God could cause a miracle conversion *a la* the Prophet Jonah and Nineveh; or, the miracle of when God ordered Ezekiel to prophecy over the dead bones that then came together as he was prophesying — however, Ezekiel at least had bones to "work" with.

What can a priest/pastor do when there is a congregation with a contraceptive/sterilization mentality? Should he tell them to repent and have a reversal of the vasectomy or tubal ligation? If that fails, should he encourage his flock to adopt or become foster parents? Should he not be promoting Natural Family Planning which uses the best of science to help couples to be fruitful–not to mention e c o l o g i c a l   b r e a s t f e e d i n g   (c f . http://www.NFPandmore.org)?

Of course, he should be doing all of these remedies and more, but at the very least he should be doing what the Curé de Ars, St. John Vianney did: fast, pray, eat potatoes for his people, his sheep. Take note that the Bishops of Great Britain have returned to Friday abstinence from meat as a corporate witness to bodily discipline and penance. Priests should be personally doing at least this much. (In the U.S., few even know that the guideline is that we should offer something up on Fridays, not necessarily meat.) Could something like what happened in England happen in the U.S.?

Cardinal Burke says not to wait for a national statement. In an exclusive interview with his Eminence, Rome correspondent for LifeSiteNews.com (April 23, 2013) Hilary White reported that, "The bishops of the world must, as individuals, take the lead in combating the Culture of Death, and not wait for the national conferences." Further, she quotes his Eminence as saying that,

> "It should be emphasized that the individual bishop has a responsibility in this matter. Sometimes what happens is the individual bishops are unwilling to do anything because they wait for the national bishops' conference to take the lead."

Well stated your Eminence! Amen, alleluia!

Perhaps his Eminence had in mind then Bp. Sample of Marquette, MI (now the Archbishop of Portland, OR.) who wrote in 2011 against the contraceptive mentality for his diocese; or, Archbishop John Myers' September 25, 2012 Pastoral Letter entitled, "When Two Become One: Pastoral Teaching on the Definition, Purpose and Sanctity of Marriage." Or perhaps he was thinking of my bishop, Bishop Jenky, C.S.C. of Peoria, IL., who in 2012, brought in Fr. McCaffrey of Natural Family Planning Outreach for the diocese's Assemble Days for Priests. In any event, Cardinal Burke could have further observed that many priests wait until their bishops say something, but, let us not disregard the impact of a corporate witness of a common statement against a common evil. We do have the precedent of Pope Pius XI.

Recall, how in the midst of the rising evil of the National Socialist Party in Germany of the 1930's, Pope Pius XI delivered to the German flock a German Encyclical, *Mit Brennender Sorge*. Read out loud during Palm Sunday Masses on March 14. 1937, Pope Pius XI addressed and condemned the racial Nazi ideology which would later lead the German government to exterminate "undesirables" such as the Jews and Gypsies. The Pope also called upon the faithful Catholics to hold fast to their Christian Faith and to the Natural Law! He reminds all Pastors of souls that,

"The priest's first loving gift to his neighbors is to serve truth and refute error in any of its forms. Failure on this score would be not only a betrayal of God and your vocation, but also an offense against the real welfare of your people and country." (#36)

How true these words are today in the face of a runaway chain reaction expanding the Culture of Death throughout all parts of society and media. It is all of a piece against the Natural Law; from contraception, sterilization, abortion, euthanasia, to the acceptance of homosexual and heterosexual sodomy within and without a "marriage" relationship. We are indeed in need of a new *Mit Brennender Sorge* moment for our day! A Catholic moment not for one country or people, but for the universal Church at large. An encyclical letter that would be read out at all churches on the same weekend.

It has been reported that Pope Francis is going to complete the incomplete encyclical of Pope Emeritus Benedict XVI on Faith; would that his second encyclical (if his Holiness is open to suggestions) be on the defense of the Natural Law – *Humanae Vitae 2.0*. I would hope that he would use Pope Benedict XVI's wonderful address on the Natural Law that he gave to the German Parliament, Bundestag in September of 2011 as a start. If I may further presume to offer that the encyclical be centered on Jesus Christ and Him Crucified and how the Natural Law can be obscured in one's heart in a variety of ways (cf. St. Thomas Aquinas, *Summa Theologiae*, I-II q.94, 6 art. & q. 77) *viz.* passion, evil persuasion, vicious custom, self-rationalization, corrupt habits, and unnatural vices (*cf.* Romans 1, homosexual acts). While civil law acts as a moral guide (St. Thomas), it is not infallible, and there can, in fact, be evil laws–which Aquinas calls not laws, but "a perversion of law." Again, think of the laws under Nazi Germany then or now with many U.S. states pushing for homosexual "marriages." I would also impose or extend the impediment to Holy Orders to any man seeking to become a permanent deacon: if he has been sterilized he should not be ordained. This and other things could be done which would announce to the encroaching secular world: "Thus far and no more–not within our One, Holy, Catholic, and Apostolic Church!"

Again, I do not know how to defuse the current demographic bomb we are collectively riding. While the Church does challenge faithful Catholics to be open to life and to be fruitful in having children; something serious needs to be done. I believe Church historians will look back at this period of the post-Vatican II era and call it by some moniker–please LORD let it not be an unfortunate one. Whatever this period will be called it seems like we, as the Church, are living through a mass protest revolution; albeit perhaps unconscious, and perhaps unthinking, but we have done so, willingly. The flock is listening to a deceptive voice of a deceiving shepherd when it comes to not having many children or keeping with sexual purity.

My purpose with this article is not to throw stones, but to have an honest discussion regarding the state of the Church—"a voice in the desert." At the beginning of his pontificate Pope Emeritus Benedict XVI said, "The Church as a whole and all her Pastors, like Christ, must set out to lead people out of the desert, towards the place of life, towards friendship with the Son of God, towards the One who gives us life, and life in abundance." (Mass of Imposition of the Pallium, April 24, 2005) He repeated these words in his opening to this Year of Faith. (*cf. Porta Fidei*, Oct. 11, 2012) As shepherds and pastors of souls, priests and bishops must be willing to cast our nets in waters that may seem un-safe or unwelcoming. But if we do not go out into the deep, we may find that the shallows have all been fished out. Yes, pastors must open the Doors of Faith, but we ourselves must be willing to walk in first. If we, the shepherds, are unwilling to defend the Natural Law against the onslaught of secularism, how can we expect the flock to do so? The experience of closing and now razing a school is one I do not want to repeat. For if a bishop or a priest hates closing a school, he is really going to hate closing a parish. In the midst of this Year of Faith, let us pray to the Holy Spirit to lead us out of this desert, this demographic winter, into a new Springtime and may Our Lady, the undoer of knots, open up our hearts to the love of God the Father and His Son, Jesus, and the love of new life in the Holy Spirit. Amen!

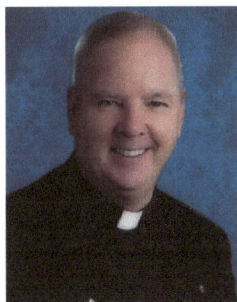

Fr. Timothy Sauppé, S.T.L. is pastor of St. Mary's Church, Westville, Illinois, in the Diocese of Peoria.

The Bellarmine Forum was delighted delighted to welcome his contribution and looks forward to more from this good priest "in the trenches."

KABOOM!
The Literary Finale of Pope Benedict XVI was not his abdication.
by John B. Manos

Posted on February 13, 2013

By now, anyone who reads this has heard of the surprise and seemingly sudden abdication of the Seat of Peter by Pope Benedict XVI this past Monday. I've intentionally waited a few days for it all to sink in before interpreting what happened. If there is one thing I've admired about Pope Benedict is his capacity to speak fully in the literal sense and in that secondary, albeit equally important, symbolic or literary sense. It took at least a few days for all the noise to quiet down so that enough information about the facts could be available to see if in fact Pope Benedict had a literary message for his finale. Turns out he did — a shocker at that!

Like a great composer, such as Tchaikovsky, I would have been disappointed had it not been there. The 1812 Overture has so many details buried within it that it seems as if I can enjoy it brand new over and over. The same can be said of Dostoevsky, it took years for me to figure out why Raskolnikov stepped over the threshold. There was the literal sense – he in fact walked into a room. The literary sense had much more meaning. Today, the Internet is full of essays about what that literary symbolism meant, so much that cliches abound. The expectation is clear however, that I knew to expect something literary from Pope Benedict. Like his term *dehellenization* coined at the Regensberg Lecture, I knew Pope Benedict would have woven meaning into this very significant event. In fact, I'm convinced there is more, but today we have a big piece of the finale message of Pope Benedict.

Like all literary things, however, culture and context converge that we may focus on aspects of literary symbols, but there is never enough to be said. Literary symbols, after all, are composite pictures — if one picture is worth a thousand words, then the literary symbols, as composites, would manifest millions of words. To set context and capture at least one sense of Pope Benedict's finale, we must set the stage.

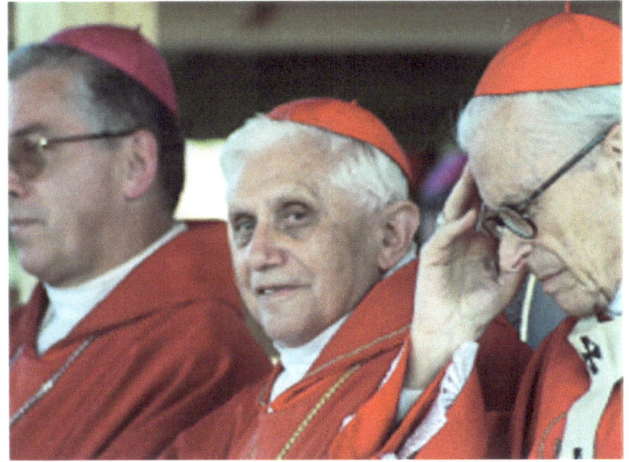

Far from the seemingly ordinary business of making saints, Pope Benedict called a consistory of the cardinals to canonize three cases of saints. Three that he selected from the pile of thousands of cases finished and ready for canonization. My sources, that I believe to be reliable, tell me that there are roughly 2000 cases of cause investigations that have been completed are are awaiting advancement to adjudication by the cardinal college as to whether these may be canonized. From that pile, it is the charge of the Holy Father to select and advance each case to the cardinals. Thus, it was Pope Benedict's prerogative to weave his finale using the stories and lives of these cases to make a literary statement, should he choose to do so. Much like the 1812 Overture, one of these three cases is a surprise! It is like the cannons. It is that striking and far more dramatic than any mere statement he could have made with words.

This case is even more striking than the lightning bolt that hit St. Peter's as the Pope spoke Latin in precise terms indicating, as a musical score, fine. It's this music on the line before the fine that we need to hear – it was the canonization of Blessed Antonio Primaldo and his 799 companions, the Martyrs of Otranto. As I continue to read this account, I am not only flabbergasted at the story itself, but I find myself coming back and back to extract more and more bits of literary message from Pope Benedict.

Let me just say, that I believe Pope Benedict may have said more in this one act than all of his obvious writings may have said. It's just that rich and meaty.

I will borrow from someone else's synopsis of the cause. The blog *Ex Umbria et Imaginibus* reported the cause on Feb 4. I am borrowing whole cloth here, and note my appreciation for the succinct synopsis there:

> Blessed Antonio was a tailor, a man advanced in years we are told, when the city was invaded by Muslims in 1480. The men of the city were promised their lives if they converted to Islam, but encouraged by Blessed Antonio, they remained firm. After the fall of the city following a brutal siege, they barricaded themselves into the cathedral and prepared for martyrdom. The siege and this further inconvenience for the Muslims actually helped save Italy as news of the invasion had time to get out and armies could prepare for battle as the Turks tried to ferret out the men. In the end, the cathedral was breached, and the men taken to the Hill of Minerva where they were all beheaded. According to one account a Catholic priest helped the Turks and tried to persuade the men to abandon their Christian faith.[1]

A contemporary document reports what happened, singling Blessed Antonio out for his heroism. Here is an extract:

> And turning to the Christians, Primaldo spoke these words: 'My brothers, until today we have fought in defence of our homeland, to save our lives, and for our earthly governors; now it is time for us to fight to save our souls for our Lord. And since he died on the cross for us, it is fitting that we should die for him, remaining firm and constant in the faith, and with this earthly death we will earn eternal life and the glory of martyrdom.' At these words, all began to shout with one voice and with great fervour that they wanted to die a thousand times, by any sort of death, rather than renounce Jesus Christ.

Antonio, for his obstinacy was the first to die, but accounts say his headless body refused to fall to the ground and remained standing until the last person had been martyred despite attempts by Muslim soldiers to pull it to the ground. As another account relates:

> All of them repeated their profession of the faith and the generous response they had given at first, so the tyrant commanded that the decapitation should proceed, and, before the others, the head of the elderly Primaldo should be cut off. Primaldo was hateful to him, because he never stopped acting as an apostle toward his fellows. And before placing his head upon the stone, he told his companions that he saw heaven opened and the comforting angels; that they should be strong in the faith and look to heaven, already open to receive them. He bowed his head and it was cut off, but his corpse stood back up on its feet, and despite the efforts of the butchers, it remained erect and unmoving, until all were decapitated. The marvelous and astonishing event would have been a lesson of salvation for those infidels, if they had not been rebels against the light that enlightens every man who lives in the world. Only one of the butchers, named Berlabei, believed courageously in the miracle and, declaring himself a Christian in a loud voice, was condemned to be impaled.

This, this, my brothers in Christ, is what Pope Benedict made as his finale! Can you hear the cannons of the overture? They sound weak next to Pope Benedict's finale, don't they? There is so much information there!

I believe a multivolume treatise can unpack this story

---

[1] Excerpt from the blog post at
http://fatherdirector.blogspot.com/2013/02/eight-hundred-and-two-new-saints-on-way.html (*last retrieved February 13, 2013*).

and there be much left to say. For instance, that Antonio was a tailor makes me think of Pope Pius X, whose family name Sarto means tailor. Or, the concept that the pope as Vicar for Jesus Christ, is the head of the visible Church, the rest of us Her body. What do you make of the account that although Antonio had been decapitated, the body stood erect and the murderers could not take it down?

Looking past the literal elements of the invaders, and taking instead note of the location — on the hill of Minerva. Minerva was the Roman pagan goddess of wisdom (analogue of Greek Athena). As the daughter of Jupiter, she was worshipped throughout the Roman Empire. Her pagan feast day was five days after the Ides of March. Among everything else that can be said, was it the case that Pope Benedict saw the gnostic goddess of wisdom's worship as the place at which the head is decapitated?

Even in the names of Antonio's companions–one of them, the Archbishop, is named Agricoli (*lit.* "Farmers"). Is he perhaps symbolic of the average guy being pushed out by the dehellenized sophisticates of our day? The sophisticated, slick, and attractively packaged types who seem no longer able to apprehend objective reality. Those who, by their fashion to mammon and worship of perception, overlook the farmer's wisdom and would kill them off?

Do you see what I mean? There's so much here that we could talk for years and have more to discuss. Thank you Pope Benedict!

I want however, to leave this idea on the most solid message I see in it. Pope Benedict seems to be telling us that the Heavens are opened and we must stand firm in our faith!

Without even the benefit of a few days to digest the literary BOOM, it appears that Cardinal Arinze had heard the same message, but this video clip of his statement speaks for itself. Note well that Cardinal Arinze heard the cannons, too, although he said it as thunder. KABOOM!

Viva il papa! For now, that's only one of the three cases he selected. The other two are nuns, and we'll look at them soon enough. Enjoy the cannons!

Jesus wasn't good enough for them either, Pope Francis, S.J.

by John B. Manos

Posted on March 15, 2013

When Pope Francis walked out on the balcony yesterday, I watched and listened as best I could to his Italian. I understood the part where he said they found him at the end of the world, and then I understood his first act: asking everyone to pray for Pope Emeritus Benedict, and then doing so with an Our Father, Hail Mary, and Glory Be.

(we'll read what happened when Jesus was on the balcony before the people in a couple weeks).

Thanks be to God. That raucous crowd of people hushed down from primal cheers into prayer. The crowd's cheering had been like Palm Sunday all over again. He tamed them and brought them to God in one quick act. Instantly, he was like John the Baptist, who told us "He must increase; I must decrease." This Pope managed to shift the focus to God, and not on the generic celebrity simulacrum infused with cheerful emotion.

Then, in a move that reminded me of Father Hardon, who began anything with his typical command: "Suppose we start with a Prayer." Pope Francis then asked the tamed crowd to pray for him. I watched the TV coverage and the people were praying.

Father Hardon would then commend the act to the Blessed Mother. This pious and commended practice is an unnoticed Jesuit characteristic. Most people recognize AMDG (*ad maiorem Dei gloriam*) but only the more attentive can recall the second act, BVMH, let alone recite its meaning: to the honor of the Blessed Virgin Mary (for the record, just a couple weeks ago, Mr. Dejak and I were bantering this very point about on Facebook). Thus, the habit of a well-formed Jesuit, such as Fr. Hardon, is to first pray to God for the grace, and then recommend the results to the honor of His Mother. St. Ignatius and St. Xavier would have it no other way.

It is thus a pattern I recognize, thanks in large part to Fr. Hardon and a few other Jesuits along the way. The next thing I saw Pope Francis do was to mention that he intended to visit the Blessed Mother today. If it would have been possible, I bet he would

have done so right then. But his mention of it in this sequence spoke volumes to me.

Then, only then, after having adequately prepared for his endeavor, did he proceed to begin the work of Pope. He put his stole on and imparted the *Urbi et Orbi* apostolic blessing. I was sold right there. Pope Francis had shown that he is willing to bring the habits he learned in his formation in the rule of the Society of Jesus to bear. He is willing to accept the grace now proper to him as Pope. Whatever else he has been, only now will he get the graces God needs him to have to be Pope. Starting in the manner he did gives me a sign that he intends to cooperate with that grace. It showed in the reaction of the crowd.

From Palm Sunday to Good Friday in only a couple hours (not even days)

A couple of hours later, I read the mess on *Rorate Ceoli*, a blog frequented by sedevacantists, SSPXers, and traditional Mass goers. I confess, having grown up with a rogue Dominican rite latin Mass that was later made into a 1962 Missal, and later latin, but always chanted Mass, that I read the stuff there a lot. There's a reason I don't join the Amish clubs they tend to attract and make soap, though: they have in many ways lost their sense of Jesus and reduced the faith to externals. Not able to comprehend what they just saw happen, they had to start with the sowing of doubt. You might as well say that the tenor of the comments might as well have been cries, "Crucify him! Crucify him!"

The Pharisees did this sowing of doubt based on nonsense, too. Of Our Lord, they said He was a drunkard (winebibber), that He hung out with hookers, that His apostles failed to keep the rites and practices properly (such as washing their hands the right way), or even that He broke God's law by healing people on the Sabbath (I'm sorry but that still cracks me up — the hubris of these idiots). What I found most strange was that it happened within hours. You'd think they would have at least waited for the Ides of March, that famous day of Roman history when the leader gets stabbed in the back by his best men. No, they had to jump on the case and be first out of the gate.

Then, today, I see Pope Francis take flowers to the Blessed Mother and leave them for her. I also read his homily (*see below*). If you haven't read the homily yet, or heard others praise it for having a sharp edge like the words of Christ, go read it for yourself. It outlines what he intends, and he's onto a good path. (I do hope he causes the USCCB to revert to translations of Holy Scripture that have language as clear as his, not the tripe we are force-fed at Holy Mass… after all, what good is the latin if the readings used are vacated of sense and meaning? but that's another discussion for another day).

Throughout the day, however, I have seen more and more "Important Catholics" not just the traditionalists coming out with the daggers and sowing doubts. I refuse to link to these idiots. You'll see it being passed along. I will however, acknowledge a post on this very topic from Dr. Taylor Marshall. All I can say to him is, welcome to the club — this has been my complaint for decades now. When Dr. Marshall comes to the realization that I did years ago, that Jesus Himself appearing to them would not satisfy them, he will have arrived.

Today's Gospel Says it All

This very point comes from the reading of the Mass Gospel, today, however (John 5 31-47). Even the inane translation employed by the USCCB from the ICEL (which I am convinced stands for *Inflectere Christus Ex Liturgiam*) makes enough sense to convey the point: God Himself was not good enough for the Pharisees — they were more important than Him. In it Jesus declares:

> Moreover, the Father who sent me has testified on my behalf.
> But you have never heard his voice nor seen his form,
> and you do not have his word remaining in you,
> because you do not believe in the one whom he has sent.
> […]

I know that you do not have the love of God in you.
I came in the name of my Father, but you do not accept me;

Jesus didn't do things the Pharisees expected. His Vicar, Pope Francis, apparently doesn't either. I heard people complain that he didn't have his pectoral cross on, that he didn't chant the blessing, that he didn't act papal. There's a lot more. All of it is supposed to be a sign that he's going to be an awful pope. It's like the people of Jesus's time — they said Jesus couldn't be the Messiah because the real Messiah would do [X]. [X] was whatever image they projected on God. Some wanted a politician to remove the Romans. Jesus didn't do that, so they refused to believe Jesus was God. Others wanted a super-pharisee. Jesus wasn't a normal pharisee, so they didn't believe He was the Messiah. The lists went on. It was so bad that Jesus had to laugh in His sleeve when he asked Peter who the people said He was and none of the answers were "God." In fact, people said everything but– they said Moses, Elijah, etc… In other words, they gave Him a nice title to be polite, politeness isn't always charitable, but they refused to admit who He was.

Doesn't God Have Anything to Do with this?

Sadly, they do that to the Pope now, the Vicar of Jesus. They want him to do [X]. They aren't willing to wait and see what God will have Him do, what God wants to do for His Church through the Pope. Instead, they are already declaring him to be a disappointment. The Pope hasn't even been pope 24 hours! Given today's reading, I can't help but to think that Pope Francis really is like Jesus in that his own reject him and insult him. I'm glad he prayed for grace from the start, as it appears that this Pope's cross is coming from his own people.

For now, however, all this doubt sowing is ill-warranted and frankly borders on suspicion, as in the sin of suspicion. It's sad that he's been pope a little over a day and he's already getting chewed up. Are Catholics that ignorant of God's power today? They all talk about grace and talk like they know how to get it — could they not see that this Pope actually does it? Don't you think God will tap him on the shoulder if he's supposed to do something better? That's why we pray for the Pope. Instead, it appears people are griping about his future pontificate on his first day as Pope — no wonder this pope is already being declared as the Pope of charity! Apparently, we really need a Pope to teach us that!

FIRST HOMILY OF POPE FRANCIS

In these three readings I see that there is something in common: it is movement. In the first reading, movement is the journey [itself]; in the second reading, movement is in the up-building of the Church. In the third, in the Gospel, the movement is in [the act of] profession: walking, building, professing.

Walking: the House of Jacob. "O house of Jacob, Come, let us walk in the light of the Lord." This is the first thing God said to Abraham: "Walk in my presence and be blameless." Walking: our life is a journey and when we stop, there is something wrong. Walking always, in the presence of the Lord, in the light of the Lord, seeking to live with that blamelessness, which God asks of Abraham, in his promise.

Building: to build the Church. There is talk of stones: stones have consistency, but [the stones spoken of are] living stones, stones anointed by the Holy Spirit. Build up the Church, the Bride of Christ, the cornerstone of which is the same Lord. With [every] movement in our lives, let us build!

Third, professing: we can walk as much we want, we can build many things, but if we do not confess Jesus Christ, nothing will avail. We will become a pitiful NGO, but not the Church, the Bride of Christ. When one does not walk, one stalls. When one does not built on solid rocks, what happens? What happens is what happens to children on the beach when they make sandcastles: everything collapses, it is without consistency. When one does not profess Jesus Christ – I recall the phrase of Leon Bloy – "Whoever does not pray to God, prays to the devil." When one does not profess Jesus Christ, one professes the worldliness of the devil.

Walking, building-constructing, professing: the thing, however, is not so easy, because in walking, in building, in professing, there are sometimes shake-ups – there are movements that are not part of the path: there are movements that pull us back.

This Gospel continues with a special situation. The same Peter who confessed Jesus Christ, says, "You are the Christ, the Son of the living God. I will follow you, but let us not speak of the Cross. This has nothing to do with it." He says, "I'll follow you on other ways, that do not include the Cross." When we walk without the Cross, when we build without the Cross, and when we profess Christ without the Cross, we are not disciples of the Lord. We are worldly, we are bishops, priests, cardinals, Popes, but not disciples of the Lord.

I would like that all of us, after these days of grace, might have the courage – the courage – to walk in the presence of the Lord, with the Cross of the Lord: to build the Church on the Blood of the Lord, which is shed on the Cross, and to profess the one glory, Christ Crucified. In this way, the Church will go forward.

My hope for all of us is that the Holy Spirit, that the prayer of Our Lady, our Mother, might grant us this grace: to walk, to build, to profess Jesus Christ Crucified. Amen.

Franciscus

Why People Don't Get Pope Francis: He's Too Traditional

by John M. DeJak

Posted on August 13, 2013

I will admit to an immediate apprehension when the media takes an especial liking to a particular Catholic bishop or even the pope. I am even more apprehensive when I see a prelate "ham it up" for the cameras, never miss an opportunity to speak to some media outlet, or look like he is taking a bit too much pleasure in sipping a cocktail with a local politician or big-wig businessman. I have the opposite reaction, when I see a priest unassumingly have a beer with some dock workers (*ala'* Karl Malden in On the Waterfront) or load up a Ford F-150 with some cut wood to bring to a family with 15 kids in his parish. Pope Francis seems to be in the latter category and that's why I like him so much. Of course, as the common Father to us all and as a head of state he necessarily

has to mingle with the power elite, but it's obvious to me that he prefers associating with those who don't merit admission to that club.

The great thing about Pope Francis is that he eschews any "club" other than that of Christ and His Church. This is why secular people don't get him. It is continually interesting to see the political terms "right" and "left" being applied to the Church and to the pope. But Francis defies these designations in a most interesting way. I saw an article last week from a blog entitled The African Distributist that in a few words captured the "radicalism of Pope Francis."

"Radicalism" for the media and the current power elites is a time-bound term that refers to the mid-1960s to the early 1970s where so-called women's

rights, civil rights, and anti-authoritarianism were the order of the day. I would suggest that the common thread with all of these movements then and in their current incarnations is an intentional breaking with tradition and a practical atheism. This is not to say that there weren't injustices brought to light by these movements that in some cases needed to be remedied; but the movements, as a whole, had as their aim the uprooting of the common inheritance of the West. As proof of this philosophical, cultural, and religious *non serviam* we see these people call themselves "radical"—which is anything but getting back to the roots of things. Rather it is a chronological snobbery of the most recent vintage.

For the more thoughtful, the realization of injustices to be remedied did not mean the overthrow of the past. Indeed, it may mean the pruning of the tree of tradition from alien entanglements that have attached themselves, but it did not mean cutting it down. "Radicalism," as any intelligent and tradition-minded individual will understand, means getting to the root of things. For Pope Francis it means very simply—getting to the bare-bones truth of man and his relationship to God. "When the Son of Man comes, will He find any faith left on the earth?" A sobering question. The Holy Father, in taking a less academic tack than his predecessors, is showing a "radicalism" as to the most fundamental questions of our existence. In this he shows himself to be a true son of St. Ignatius.

The first and fundamental starting point for St. Ignatius in his spiritual teaching is that "man was created to know, love, and serve God in this world so as to be happy with Him forever in the next." As a corollary, all created realities are to help man achieve this goal—if they do not, they are to be removed. As St. Ignatius says: "We are to use creatures insofar as they help us attain our eternal end, and we are to be rid of them insofar as they prove a hindrance on our road to salvation."

Pope Francis speaks like an old parish priest to his parishioners and, as Ignatius advises, he is radically unconcerned with what people think of him or the material pomps of the papacy. In characterizing him

this way, I am not comparing him to his predecessors or criticizing his predecessors. Far from it. I rather see a pope, steeped in a time-tested and time-honored tradition of spirituality playing it out on a grand scale as the Vicar of Christ in an age that needs it more than previous ones. Furthermore, in practicing this radical indifference, he allows himself to—in the words of the Baptist—"decrease, while Christ increases."

As this Pope has unsettled the more traditional elements of the Church, perhaps he is doing them a service. Perhaps he is showing the way that our faith is in Christ, not modern comforts or an idealized notion of the Church's prestige and power. A pope who has gotten to roots is the one who speaks simply and clearly on the following: the necessity to be humble before Christ; the necessity of keeping both Christ and His Church at the center of our lives; the necessity of intercession of Our Lady; and the necessity to realize that our lives are a cosmic battle between Our Blessed Lord and the Devil. One doesn't get more fundamental, nay, traditional than that. In this lies Pope Francis's radicalism.

Perhaps the reason why people don't understand the pope is because they're not traditional enough.

No Holiness In Dissension From the Pope

by John M. DeJak

Posted on August 2, 2013

Recent days have seen much media attention focused upon the words and person of the Holy Father, Pope Francis. Not a little bit of this commentary has been disconcerting, not only from those who would twist his words to fit a secular agenda, but also from those who are supposedly faithful but seem to want to instruct the pope on how to "pope." It is unfortunate that, in this day and age, when the Church must be strong and united against the secular and, frankly, demonic forces at work in the world we have Catholics willing to tear down the pope because he is not made in their image and likeness. There seems to be a type of "subtle Protestantism" that sees the substitution of one's private judgment for that of divinely established office of the Roman Pontiff.

Of course distinctions must be made. I will trust my own wits to that of the pope if he declares that the Cubs are going to win the World Series. But regarding matters that touch upon faith and morals, we are to give him our "religious submission of intellect and will" (*Lumen Gentium*, 25). Blessed John Paul II elaborated on this point in an address to American bishops on December 6, 2004, indicating that a teaching of the "authentic Magisterium…upon a matter of faith and morals," even if not proclaimed "by definitive act," must be given "religious submission of intellect and will," requiring the faithful to "avoid whatever does not accord" with it. Indeed, even to the decisions made by the pope for the governance of the Church and her ordering, we are to show a filial obedience. These distinctions are important and the right use of our intellect is a must in these matters. Yet, there arises, not infrequently, today a mentality that will split hairs with scholastic exactitude as to the bare minimum that is required for one to be loyal to the pope. This mentality can, in some instances, lead towards a schismatic trajectory . Now, do not misunderstand, I am not calling for a cult to the pope nor a fideistic attitude. But what is needed and demanded by our Catholic Faith is a recognition of his authority, docility to his teaching, and the courage to accept the Supreme Magisterium's teaching whole and entire.

One cannot separate Christ from the Church He established. In other words, one cannot have Christ without the Church, and one cannot have the Church without Christ. Per the divine institution, the locus of authority on earth is the Roman Pontiff. The person of the Pope, willed by Christ Himself, is an essential and visible sign of the universal authority of Christ. It is unfortunate that the mentality that I speak of occurs not only with the usual suspects (i.e., materialists, rationalists, secularists, etc.) but also among those who would be considered among the faithful. Two current examples: certain Catholic blogs continue in a posture of attempting to unmask a tradition-minimizing Papa Bergoglio by pointing out that he eschews the trappings of the papal office or prefers the Roman Missal of 1970 (see an early commentary on this: "*Jesus Wasn't Good Enough for them Either, Pope Francis*" earlier in this text); the musings of a popular and learned Catholic commentator on Pope Benedict XVI's encyclical *Caritas in Veritate*, where he presumed to explicate for the faithful what in the encyclical was worthy of assent and what was debatable. Indeed, this commentator's arrogance went so far as to compare the document to "a duck-billed platypus." Hardly the words of one who shows docility to the Supreme Magisterium. This is not to say that there cannot be debate, argument, comment, and a seeking to understand the words and decisions of the Roman Pontiff. The faithful should; but they should in a way that gives reverence to his person and office and in a forum that would not further the erosion of the faith and an indifference to authority. Docility to the pope is docility to Christ.

It is human nature to have favorites and preferences, but a basic principle of our faith is that the deposit of the faith doesn't change as the Church is guaranteed divine protection and assistance. A legitimate question that might be posed is whether the standard that we follow is one that rests on this conviction, or one that is of our own judgment as how a pope ought to "pope." Frank Sheed put it well:

Our faith is rooted in Christ, not in the human instruments he uses. In a given age, a Catholic might revere the reigning pope and rejoice in his policies, and this would be an extra stimulation. On the other hand, he might find the pope's life disedifying or his policies unpleasing: and that would be depressing. But whether the pope's personality and policy stimulate him or depress him, the substance of our Catholicity is something distinct from them: what primarily matters is what we find in the Church of which the pope is the earthly ruler—the grace of the sacraments, the offering of the Sacrifice, the certitude of the truth, the unity of the Fellowship, and Christ, in whom all these are. (*Theology and Sanity*, p. 309-310)

In the end, are we striving for holiness or striving to win an argument? Maybe Pope Francis is making people uncomfortable just as Pope Benedict XVI similarly made people uncomfortable—to call them back to the fundamental truth of our existence and where our faith ought to be. Perhaps Catholics of all walks of life—myself included—ought to take to heart the words of St. Pius X:

Therefore, when we love the Pope, there are no discussions regarding what he orders or demands, or up to what point obedience must go, and in what things he is to be obeyed; when we love the Pope, we do not say that he has not spoken clearly enough, almost as if he were forced to repeat to the ear of each one the will clearly expressed so many times not only in person, but with letters and other public documents; we do not place his orders in doubt, adding the facile pretext of those unwilling to obey – that it is not the Pope who commands, but those who surround him; we do not limit the field in which he might and must exercise his authority; one does not oppose to the Pope's authority that of others, however learned they may be, who differ from him. For however great their learning, they must be lacking in holiness, for there can be no holiness in dissension from the Pope. (Pope St. Pius X, allocution of 18 November 1912, AAS vol. 4 (1912), 695).

Our job, as commanded by Christ, is to love God and love one another. In this consists holiness. Part of this means being docile to the pope and his authority–and loving him too!

Explaining Common Core: And why you don't want this in your schools

by Stephanie Block

Posted on June 19, 2013

The topics of Outcome Based Education (OBE) and national education standards were particularly explosive during the 1990s when the public first began to understand the direction progressives were taking education. Largely thanks to the whistle-blowing of people like Charlotte Iserbyt[1], there developed pockets of resistance. States, if they were able to refuse the substantial financial incentives offered for their compliance, could opt out of this problematic new education system.

Fast forward to 2009. The National Governors Association and the Council of Chief State School Officers had formed the Common Core State Standards Initiative to develop a set of English language arts and mathematics standards for the country. Still theoretically voluntary (all but five states – Alaska, Virginia, Texas, Wisconsin, and Nebraska – are implementing the standards), if a state adopts the standards, they replace any local curriculum.

Aside from disliking the one-size-fits-all nature of national standards, a number of groups have tackled the enterprise of explaining why a federal takeover of every local school system, public or private, secular or parochial, is not in the best interests of the United States...and of looking deeply into the agenda of these standards.

In Oklahoma, three women – Jenni White, Lynn Habluetzel, and Jo Joyce – have written *Common Core State Standards* and Race to the Top An Introduction to Marxism 101: Restore Oklahoma Public Education. The entire text can be read, *gratis*, in various formats by visiting the website[2].

It's quite a useful resource, providing a concise history of American public education and asking: "Since 1965, states have been given over 118 BILLION dollars (in addition to those supplied at the state/county level) through ESEA [the Elementary and Secondary Education Act] has supported a system in which 1 in 7 adults are functionally illiterate. How have we progressed from a basis of local control over local education and nearly 100% literacy rates to the point where states are signing on to a Federal initiative (to be funded by the Department of Education via 'Stimulus' {ARRA} funds) to create national educational standards (Statism)?"

The people behind this shift very intentionally – as revealed by their words and actions – are seeking the creation of a comprehensive system that addresses not merely education but job training and placement, medical care, and a host of additional social services and "benefits," managed in vast data banks that can track an individual from birth to grave. White, Habluetzel, and Joyce explain that the current federal expenditure on education (14% of the national budget) is not merely "illegal" but pushes a curriculum that has failed students over and over again.

Concluding chapters demonstrate some of the invasive aspects of this national education system,

---

[1] the website for her seminal work, *The Deliberate Dumbing Down of America*, is www.deliberatedumbingdown.com

[2] www.restoreokpubliceducation.com

COMMON CORE: WHAT'S OLD IS NEW AGAIN

WE MUST MAKE THE YOUNG INTO A GENERATION OF COMMUNISTS. CHILDREN, LIKE SOFT WAX, ARE VERY MALLEABLE AND THEY SHOULD BE MOULDED INTO GOOD COMMUNISTS... WE MUST RESCUE CHILDREN FROM THE HARMFUL INFLUENCE OF THE FAMILY... WE MUST NATIONALIZE THEM. FROM THE EARLIEST DAYS OF THEIR LITTLE LIVES, THEY MUST FIND THEMSELVES UNDER THE BENEFICIENT INFLUENCE OF COMMUNIST SCHOOLS...

TO OBLIGE THE MOTHER TO GIVE HER CHILD TO THE SOVIET STATE – THAT IS OUR TASK.

ПОД ВОДИТЕЛЬСТВОМ ВЕЛИКОГО СТАЛИНА—ВПЕРЕД К КОММУНИЗМУ!

quoting from various student questionnaires and challenging the myth of "beneficial" early childhood programs. "It IS time to REFORM education," the authors insist, "but not as a re-package of every single failed educational program since the beginning of ESEA in 1965. Education in America should affirm the ideals of American Exceptionalism as ingrained in the Constitution by our American Forefathers and expound upon the traditional methods of education that created that ideal and spawned a nation of literate, entrepreneurs and the greatest nation in 5000 years."

From St. Louis, Betsy Kraus has prepared a research report titled "Catholic Children in Grave Danger: A Report on Common Core in Catholic Schools" (the full report can be read at this link)

Kraus begins with a rather extensive list of "dangers" she sees in Common Core, including the denial of "absolute truth in God," "making all truth relative and determined by group consensus," "by-passing the free will of the child through mind control and behavioral techniques," "using a revolutionary educational system based on Marxist dialectic theory, devised by multiple continental thinkers, perfected by Transformational Marxists, and used in Soviet and U.S. classrooms," and at least a dozen others.

Nevertheless, Common Core Standards, she writes, are currently in over 100 U.S. dioceses, never mind public school districts, introduced through the Common Core Catholic Identity Initiative (CCCII) and its accompanying "National Standards and Benchmarks for Effective Catholic Elementary and Secondary Schools." "These Standards are now being incorporated into diocesan education plans under such titles as 'Pathways to Excellence', 'Mission Advancement Initiative', and 'Lighting the Way: A Vision of Catholic Education'."

Logo of the Common Core Catholic Identify Initiative [3]

Because Kraus is not so much concerned with academic success, she focuses on the consequences of "critical thinking" as a Hegelian/Marxist Dialectic designed to re-educate students from traditional to "global" values. She covers some of the same history as the Oklahomans do but is particularly concerned about modern education's philosophical threads leading toward acceptance of a totalitarian and atheistic society.

She is also at pains to contrast the broader social implications of Common Core with Catholic social teachings. To take an example, "sustainable development," an element of Common Core's package, seeks to limit human populations and eventually eliminate private property and the financial independence it insures. "Conflict resolution," another component of the Common Core package, fosters a group-think "based on religious synthesis and syncretism." One student is quoted, saying: "You can't be part of the consensus process and keep your faith in God... people learn to compromise individual beliefs and ideas in order to work for 'common goals.'...Working together as a team, (soon) using the same currency, and having the same leader(s), the same ideals, and the same minds, all over the world, is all a part of the global government that the United Nations proposes."

One marvelous section explains how students are being trained as opposed to educated. Kraus, like Charlotte Iserbyt, understand the pedagogical failure of OBE as deliberate, an effective way of producing more compliant worker for a "planned economy."

Another section, appendix-style, lists the major political players promoting Common Core and some of the political players and educators working to oppose it. Kraus offers these as an introduction to her conclusion that Catholic schools must refuse federal funding and the mandatory curricula that come with it.

Other materials: The website, Utahns Against Common Core has an extremely informative website that includes the video[4] of a clinical mental health therapist who analyzes of Common Core materials from her unique perspective. Another website, Truth in American Education[5], has links to the Common Core standards and many useful resources, including an interactive map for locating groups of other concerned citizens by state.

If you followed the national education reform movement two decades ago, you'll quickly realize that one is looking at pretty much the same package in a new wrapper. A few new names, new legislation...but the same old program. It's just as problematic now as it was then.

Ed. Note. Perusing the CCII website, and the logo above reveal that the initials themselves are CCCII. What is the fascination of these Marxists with that combination of CCCP?

CCCP Passport

---

3 the CCCII is online at http://catholicschoolstandards.org/common-core

4 www.utahnsagainstcommoncore.com/clinical-mental-health-therapist-interviewed

5 truthinamericaneducation.com

SOVIET PROPAGANDA
AND
THE MARXIST MARCH
INTO CATHOLIC SCHOOLS
BY COMMON CORE.

THEY DESCRIBE IT WELL

THE GOAL OF COMMON CORE:
BREAK THE TEACHER'S UNIONS, BRING
SOVIET PROPAGANDA
FULL CIRCLE TO REALITY

(IN USSR, THERE ARE MANY
NEW SCHOOLS BEING BUILT)

(IN THE USA, SCHOOLS
ARE CLOSING ALL THE TIME.)

(Manos says: this looks like Detroit)

COMMON CORE:
A DIALECTIC STEP
TOWARDS MAKING YOUR STUDENTS THEIRS

STALIN SAYS:
(MYOЙ
STUDENT!)ИК!

(We Grow under the Standard of Lenin & Stalin)

PARENTING LICENSES
COME TO AMERICA?

WILL OBAMACARE
BRING THEM?

A Little Catholic "Education" History: Getting Alinsky into the Catholic Parish

by Stephanie Block

Posted on June 22, 2013

Recently, while preparing an article on Common Core national standards, someone suggested that I might be interested in the "open letters" written by a group called *Catholics for Truth in Education* operating in Illinois from 1974 into the 90s. Interestingly enough, a set of these "open letters" just happened to have been sitting on my bookshelf for over a decade, waiting to be examined.

There may have been other *Catholics for Truth in Education* publications, as well, but the materials in my possession begin around the time of the first Alinskyian Call to Action conference[1] in 1976, an event that galvanized dissent within the Catholic Church of the United States and attempted to manipulate the bishops into supporting it. The ecclesial and social landscape which the "open letters" describe was chaotic, experimental, and hostile to traditional worship.

The first "open letter" examines a 1977 planning document titled the "Position Paper on Networks of Regional Parishes for Corporate Reconstruction" written by the (since deceased) industrial/organizational psychologist Dr. Robert R. Newsome.[2]

Newsome was on the cutting edge of "parish renewal." To pioneer various renewal strategies and incubate a reformed Church, he conceived of an "alliance" of Chicago parishes, the Parish Corporate Renewal Network, which would operate unmolested

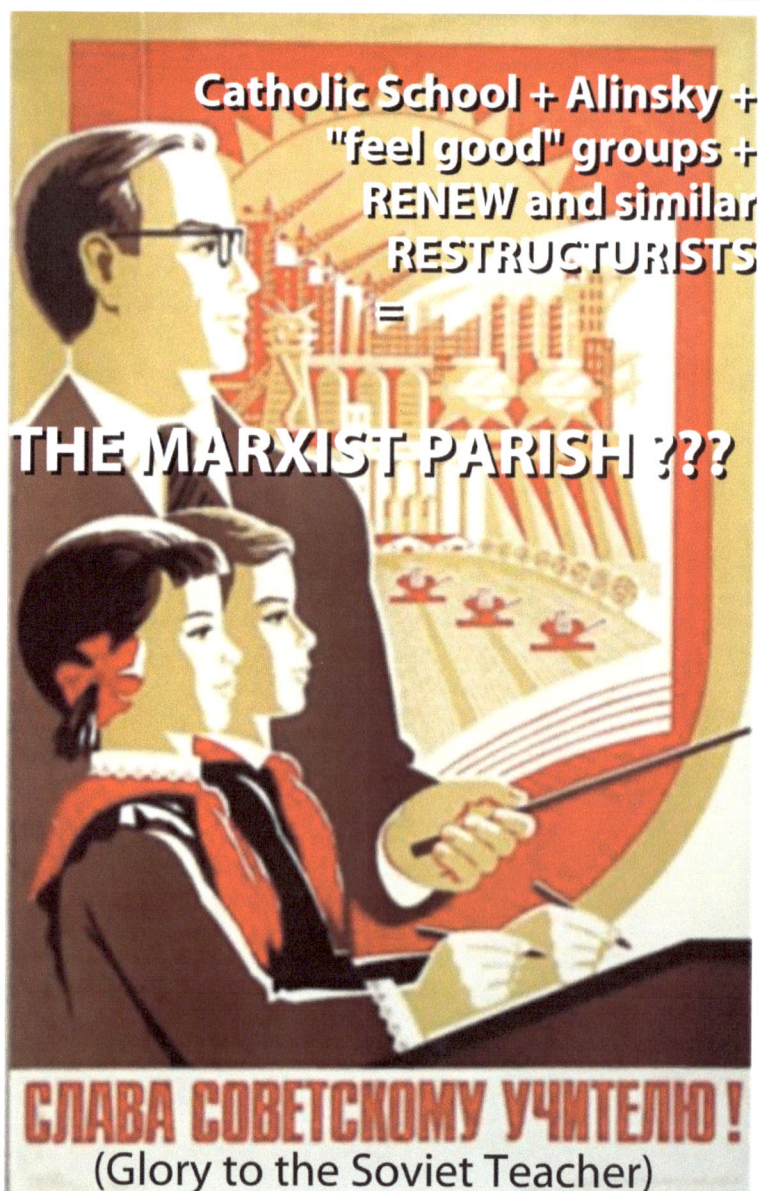

Catholic School + Alinsky + "feel good" groups + RENEW and similar RESTRUCTURISTS =

THE MARXIST PARISH ???

СЛАВА СОВЕТСКОМУ УЧИТЕЛЮ !
(Glory to the Soviet Teacher)

---

[1] For a detailed history of the relationship between Alinsky-trained clerics and the Call to Action dissenting movement in the US Catholic Church, see "Underground Call to Action:" www.catholicculture.org/culture/library/view.cfm?id=1318

[2] Robert R. Newsome also wrote a book, The Ministering Parish: Methods And Procedures for Pastoral Organization, Paulist Press, 1982

until other structures replaced it. A 1977 request grant request for the network wrote that:

> "the project faces a challenge of dramatically changing the way Catholic parishes serve themselves and the secular community of which they are a part. Heretofore, parishes have principally focused upon the salvation and grace of their members. The purpose of this project is to unleash the capacity of parishes to be apostolic organizations with a new vision, mission, and capability for developing the greatness and well-being of mankind."[3]

For a Catholic to separate "the greatness and well-being of mankind" from "salvation and grace" is quite extraordinary but Newsome proposed to accomplish it in three phases. The first targeted parish staff and created five teams of laity for re-education and training.

Once properly prepared, they would function like a virus inside the parish community, moving with "a clear, shared vision and mission" but anticipating "rejection." (page 5) Small faith communities with the unappealing title of "Corporate Reflection Centers" were to be formed throughout each parish during this next phase and each would model the new vision: "This vision of corporate man is one in which unity in diversity rather than uniformity is values."

By phase three, the parish was ready to move out into the community at large, seeking "partnership" "with all men of good will for the sake of the transformation of the urban community and the world." (page 6) Unsophisticated by today's standards, where we no longer alert people that they are to be transformed but simply launch into the process, Newsome's project was remarkably forthright.

Then, there was Msgr. John (Jack) Egan – who not only served on Saul Alinsky's Industrial Areas Foundation board but co-chaired the 1976 Call to Action conference's plenary sessions –and who also served on the Board of Advisers for the Parish Corporate Renewal Network. Incarnate in Father Egan, the elements of organized Church dissent, organized secular political activism, and a reorganized parish were intrinsically related to one another. Easy enough to see in hindsight.

Msgr. Egan writes:

> Working with parishes through my diocesan post in Chicago's Office of Urban Affairs, I saw the parish as a neighborhood institution with great potential for influence. Neighborhood issues of housing, police protection, education, availability of health services and sanitation affected the daily life of parishioners. The parish priests and people could not afford not to be involved. Citizen-parishioners along with their clergy became key actors in community organizations which not only improved the quality of life in their own neighborhoods, but had a great effect on the life of the city of Chicago.
>
> Today there are more cities in the nation boasting of strong citizen groups than ever before. Generally speaking, the growth of community organization in our urban areas has been supported both financially and morally in large measure by parishes which recognize the critical relationship between critical human problems and the dignity of persons in their neighborhoods. I would venture to say that without Church support most of the community organizations would either have been neither developed nor sustained.[4]

---

[3] "Request for Foundation Assistance from Parish Corporate Renewal Network (Internal Corporate Renewal Network)," August 1, 1977, page 1. Six foundations were approached using this document: DeRance, Inc., George Halas Foundation, Lewis Foundation, Lilly Endowment, Inc., Raskob Foundation, and the Dr. Scholl Foundation. The last of these foundations publically distanced itself from the whole business, according to "open letter #4."

[4] Msgr. John J. Egan, "Do we need parishes?" Parish Ministry, Nov-Dec 1980, pp 2-3, as quoted in Catholics for Truth in Education "open letter" #9, part 2 (June 1983).

By the second "open letter," five months later, the US bishops had responded to the 1976 Call to Action recommendations, many of which were too radical for implementation. However, a "Project for Parish Renewal" was approved as a "major priority" for every US diocese[5] and Catholics for Truth in Education watched the process, as it unfolded in Chicago, closely.

From the advantage of 35 years in the future, one can see that, for some, "renewal" was an honest endeavor. To them, it meant simply a reinvigoration of parish life that might include building new schools, improving resources, or developing ministries. For the reformers, however, "renewal" was consciously and deliberately ordered toward ideological "transformation." A transformed parish would have little resemblance to a Catholic community. The third "open letter" documents the push of various Network clergy for women and married priests, acceptance of divorce, homosexuality, and birth control, as well as belief in a non-hierarchical Church structure that was to be separated from Rome. The Network "theological adviser," a philosophy professor[6] hired to conduct talks in Chicago-area parishes about Network's vision for restructuring, is quoted spouting pure liberation theology. "Someday this world will be The Kingdom," he assures listeners. "The Kingdom is the state of affairs – the here and now."

Maybe somebody's Kingdom, but not Christ's.[7]

One gets lost in among the interconnected names and groups who are pushing this transformative, un-

Catholics for Truth in Education concludes by letter #4 that, for one thing, they are to be drawn into Alinskyian community organizations and their activism.

Catholic form of "renewal." Equally numbing are the grey, bureaucratic details that comprise this or that version of the new structure. The interesting bit, however, is where the action leads. Once parishes are restructured and "properly" retrained, what are they primed to do?

Catholics for Truth in Education concludes by letter #4 that, for one thing, they are to be drawn into Alinskyian community organizations and their activism. Letter # 9, five years later, describes an archdiocesan program structured exactly along the lines those lines, including parish listening sessions to make people "feel important" (yes, that's what the archdiocesan materials say), analysis of these sessions for purposes of developing strategic plans, provision of "theological reflection and leadership training," all aimed at ecumenical political activism. "A major part of this renewal is getting the Catholic laity involved in performing the social ministry of the Church," Dr. Newsome opines, "including the building of better neighborhoods and communities."[8] Community organizing is a means to this end.

But there are others. Letter #5 takes the reader on a romping survey of the most exciting liberationist activity at the time – which is where, oddly enough, it intersects with contemporary Common Core national standards (and why, I suspect, I was encouraged to read the "open letters"). In the middle of discussion about theological movements in Latin America and their challenges to Church teaching, the reader is introduced to a process for controlling groups of people called "Management by Objectives." (MBO)

MBO had initially been introduced into the business world as an accounting system. Like education reform pedagogy called "mastery learning" – later called "outcome based education" and still later reintroduced through the Common Core national standards – or psychology's value clarification techniques,

---

[5] "A Call to Action: Five-Year plan of Action" Origins 8, 5-28-78.

[6] The Nov.1984 "open letter" quotes this theological adviser telling his students, " We affirmed the Church is dead and found it a liberating revelation," & "Isn't being a Catholic one of the biggest blocks to being a Christian?"

[7] See John 18:36…and Romans 14: 17.

[8] Jack Houston, "'Parish renewal' project sparks a Catholic battle," Chicago Tribune, 5-31-79.

MBO was a systematic attempt to reprogram the individual's values and actions. Simply stated, the process begins with predetermined goals (or standards) to which the individual is held accountable. Of concern to Catholics for Truth in Education, several dioceses around the country were using MBO strategies as part of their pastoral planning for renewal.

Almost prescient for a time that predated a global Internet and cell phones, *Catholics for Truth in Education* worried about computerized data collection schemes that supported MBO aims. What must have seemed paranoid to most readers then has an air of prophesy to a generation that lives with the reality of government monitoring of citizens. The people who recoiled from Huxley's Brave New World couldn't have fathomed the level of invasiveness that would become possible and tolerated.

The "letters" written throughout the 1980s[9] drown the reader with descriptions of specific programs, practitioners, and tactics. So many Catholics were dancing behind the Pied Piper of "change" with little curiosity about where he was leading. *Catholics for Truth in Education* examined dozens of re-education programs in the Chicago Archdiocese – among them the once ubiquitous RENEW[10] – and explained the relationship of each to Call to Action dissent and a socialistic world view.

The end product, however, was never about the Church, not really, but about society. The Church had to be transformed so that it wouldn't be an obstacle to transforming society. *Catholics for Truth in Education* ha-

rangues about Marxist infiltration and apostasy are easy to dismiss as alarmist but, after decades of chaos, the Church in the U.S. faces serious persecution for holding on to the last shreds of Catholic integrity. The old, bureaucratic liberals, who still push their un-Catholic agendas – JustFaith and Nuns on the Bus, Alinskyian organizers and New Agers, I'm looking at you – are comfortable with that.

Historical facts are hard to dispute – and they have led to the results that are very much what Catholics for Truth in Education feared: too many Catholics who reject Church teaching. After her death, the son of Catholics for Truth in Education's founding president, Mary Catherine Davis, wrote, "The more that time passes the more things big and small I see my mother was right about."

Yes, she was.

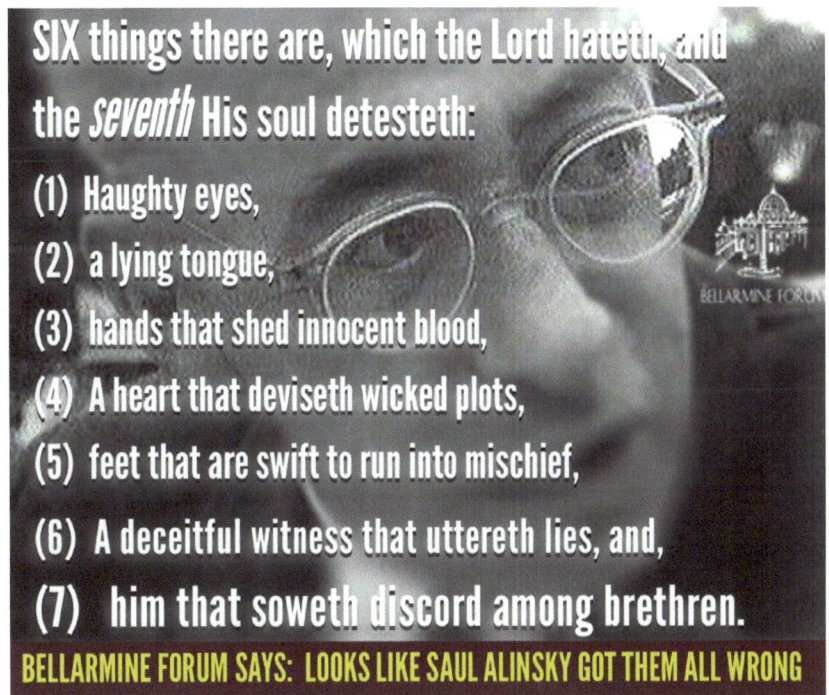

SIX things there are, which the Lord hateth, and the *seventh* His soul detesteth:
(1) Haughty eyes,
(2) a lying tongue,
(3) hands that shed innocent blood,
(4) A heart that deviseth wicked plots,
(5) feet that are swift to run into mischief,
(6) A deceitful witness that uttereth lies, and,
(7) him that soweth discord among brethren.

BELLARMINE FORUM SAYS: LOOKS LIKE SAUL ALINSKY GOT THEM ALL WRONG

Saul Alinksy, self described "Radical" devoted to Lucifer.

---

[9] "Open letters" #6-9 sport the by-line of Peter S. Newman, editor. The other issues carry no attribution.

[10] For several analyses of RENEW, see Mary Jo Anderson, "Buried in the Fine Print: An Inside Look at RENEW 2000," Crisis, March 1999; Frank Morriss' "Restructuring the Church into Their Own Image: The Link Between RENEW and the New Biblical Scholarship," Wanderer Forum Foundation Quarterly, June 1992 (also published on our website); Beth Drennan, Esq., "Background Check of RENEW 2000 Contributors Reveals RENEW 2000 Texts Laced with Call to Action Names," Women Faith and Family, 1998. Drennan has also published another discussion of the Call to Action elements found in RENEW 2000 in "Paulists' RENEW 2000 Is Just a Front for Call to Action," The Wanderer, 9-10-98.

Until the Choir Sings "Amen" – One Easy Secret to a Happy Death

by John B. Manos

Posted on November 16, 2013

"Life is a play in which for a short time one man represents a judge, another a general, and so on; after the play no further account is made of the dignity which each one had."

–St. John Chrysostom

It's that time of year when we ought to have been focused on the eleventh and twelfth articles of the Nicene Creed:

and I look forward to the resurrection of the dead and the life of the world to come.

I prefer, however, the expression of latin in *Credo IV* (as if anyone hears this anymore… but I won't digress into the sad state of Gregorian chant in America):

Et expecto resurrectionem mortuorum, et vitam ventúri sæculi.

I can still hear the pipe organ played by Don Barrett… and the rough and tumbled "Amen."

What do those words mean to you in daily life? Are Catholics meant to live differently because the day will come when Jesus will resurrect everyone from their graves?

Have <u>you</u> thought about that? We live in a world where people have a greater expectation of a zombie apocalypse — what are they saying? It's almost as if they want everyone to think that we will be zombies at the second coming. Not so! Jesus told us to expect a future life with Him, even for sinners who repent, right from the Cross!

Remember me, O Lord!

It started right on the Cross. The gospels tell us the good thief said that he deserved to die on the cross but Our Lord did not deserve such a death. Then he turned to Our Lord and said: "*Lord, remember me when Thou comest into Thy kingdom*" (*Luke* xxiii 42).

And Our Lord promised him that he would be with Him. (!)

That promise is echoed to all of us with the same simple condition: *repent*. The creed, by referencing an expectation of resurrection, reminds all of us that death, although inevitable, is not the end — Jesus made more to the story. It is the first of what St. John Chrysostom calls "the journey to eternity." He was referring to the four last things: Death, Judgment, Heaven, Hell.

Death

All men must die, because death is the consequence of original sin.

It is strange that there is discussion of so many other ways to live forever today. There's even a guy who says that by 2045, he wants to upload himself into a computer, and wants to offer the same to everyone else. Color me unimpressed. Nonplussed, even. I trust more in the Guy Who did this without a computer 2000 years ago — on the first Easter.

What does it tell us, though, that there would be so much discussion and effort towards mankind trying to make its own immortality? Several things, but the first is that everyone dies. The second is that people don't want to die. The third is that people don't understand or believe that God already made a way for us to upload our entire life, body, soul, spirit, memories, and all to a real existence! ***et expecto…***

We don't need a computer charlatan in a future development to live forever… Catholics already have the keys to that.

But let's explore this first last thing: death. What happens?

So far, there are only two people on earth that did not die when a normal life would expect it: Henoch [Enoch] (Gen. v 24) and Elias (4 Kings ii 11) BUT they are to return before the Last Day, and then they will die. So, they have only delayed the inevitable. St. Thomas Aquinas teaches that even those who survive until the Day of Judgment shall die (probably at the blast of glory that will precede His arrival). Christ alone was not under the law of death because He was free from all sin. Thus, His death for us was a purely voluntary act. Caused by Original Sin, our first parents lost by their sin the gift of immortality, and as a consequence we all have to die. "*By one man sin entered into the world and by sin death; and so death passed upon all men, in whom all have sinned*" (Rom v 12).

Death is the punishment of man's ambition to be as God. Remember that guy above who is trying to make immortality in a computer? That's right… I think he might be trying to be something he can't be. Let's hope he isn't knowingly trying to be God. But his efforts are folly.

Death is not metamorphosis, but the separation of the soul from the body

At death the soul is separated from the body, and enters the world of spirits. Meanwhile, the body decays, and falls into dust. St. Paul speaks of death as a dissolution (2 Tim iv 6), and St. Peter calls the body a tabernacle of the soul (2 Pet. i. 14). The body is, as it were, a shell through which the soul breaks to enter into its new life. St. Augustine said, "The soul is freed from its prison at death."

Remember thou art dust and to dust thou shalt return. The body, deprived of the soul, is no longer alive, because it has no longer the principle of life. At death, the spirit returns to the God Who gave it (Eccles xii 7). St. John Chrysostom therefore says, "Death is a journey into eternity." Hence it is wrong to believe with the ancient Egyptians, popularized today by shows like Ancient Aliens, or the numerous new age shysters among us, that the soul is joined to other forms, whether human or animal. For them, and for many other pagan cults, death represented some sort of metamorphosis. Even today you hear such nonsense rambled about that we can reincarnate to become something better, and repeat until perfect. Nonsense! These people, seduced by error, think perfection is something they can do to themselves. The error is subtle, but they want to be like God — to make their own eternity (sort of like that guy above and his computer). Similarly, the others around us today are mistaken who think that the soul enters into a sort of sleep until the day of judgment. No… you're going to be **VERY AWARE** — (but we'll discuss that later). After death the body returns to the dust from which it came (Gen iii 19).

(*N.B.* there are only two bodies that didn't return to dust: the bodies of Christ and of His Blessed Mother. Also, the bodies of some of the saints have been preserved free from corruption to the present day. For the Blessed Mother, her death was a sort of sleep — as tradition has referred to her death as a Dormition, which means sleep. The rest of us, well… that's the point of this post)

At the last day our bodies will all rise again. (*et expecto*!) Death is represented symbolically as a skeleton carrying a scythe, with which he cuts short our lives as the reaper mows the grass of the field (Ps cii (ciii) 14-16).

Death Reveals the Folly of the World

While here, so many people get confused as to the important things. Despite all the wealth and means, the rich man cannot take his riches along with him (Job xxvii 15). Despite whatever prestige and importance one obtains during life, Our Lord reminds us that after death many who have been the first on earth shall be last, and the last first (Matt. xix. 30). So that guy trying to upload himself into the computer may in fact be trying to preserve his importance here on earth?

Age and experience begins to reveal a different picture. Autumn after autumn show that the trees and nature understand the vanity and a fleeting one at that. Our days upon earth are but a shadow (Job viii 9). Worse yet, our years shall be considered as a spider's web and our lives are but a sigh (Ps. lxxxix (xc) 9). A sigh! No matter how many years pile up, time shows it all as but a sigh! The idea of it all being like a breath is pretty strong in the prophets. "Life is a vapor which appear for a little while, and afterwards shall vanish away" (James iv 15). As I get older, I really begin to see the wisdom in that expression! You're never really sure when the breath is out — when it's time to sing "Amen."

Death, the thief in the night

The hour of our death is unknown to us. The Gospels remind us that we shall die when we expect it not (Matt xxiv 44) but rather, death will come like a thief (id. verse 43). St. Ephrem says "death is like the pounce of the hawk, or the spring of the wolf." St. Gregory of Nyssa compares life to a torch, which a slight puff of wind may put out. Only a few saints had the hour of their death been revealed. St. Mary of Egypt, for instance, knew and prepared. They were unique, though because from almost all men it is hidden. God's wisdom and goodness hides it, or we'd be like the lazy servants the master caught (and beat, no less). Rather, since we do not know the hour of our death, we should always be ready to die!

"Wherefore be you also ready, because at what hour you know not the Son of man will come!" (Matt xxiv 44).

If you think Our Lord didn't mean that literally, then check out the parable of the ten virgins (Matt xxv). St. Ephrem commented on this though saying: "Death is a great lord waiting on no one and demanding that all wait upon him." As a man lives, so he dies. Those who put off reforming their lives are like those students who begin to study when the examination is already upon them. Thus, God hides the moment from us that we might be motivated to be ready!

There is an answer to this issue of Death

Death is terrible only to the sinner, in no wise to the just.

St. Vincent Ferrer tells us, "The death of the just man is like the pruning of a tree preparing it to bear nobler fruit in the future; while the death of the sinner is the uprooting of the tree before it is cast into the fire."

This exposition of the obvious may sound like doom and gloom to some readers, but to others, they should be nonplussed because they are already ready. In a world overcome with doomsday preparation, where it seems that everyone is getting ready for some awful events to happen, I wonder how many started at the confessional. In a world overrun with the hyper-sensual and self-seeking, only for them is death fearful because it means the end of their enjoyment and the beginning of woe. St Vincent Ferrer also said, with the quote above, "For the just man there is no death but a passing into everlasting life."

The saints rejoiced in death, desiring like St. Paul to be dissolved and to be with Christ (Phil i 23). St. John Chrysostom compares the desire of the saints for death with that of a traveller for the end of his journey, or a farmer for his harvest; in another place he speaks of death as of a change from a tumbledown cottage to a beautiful mansion. "O how sweet it is to die, if one's life has been a good one!" exclaims St. Augustine. I'm always taken aback by these quotes — are you that secure in your future?

Do you believe the *et expecto?*

If you have second thoughts, consider that it is not the kind of death, but the state of the soul that is important: "As the tree falls so shall it lie." (Eccles xi 3) and so it is with man. As his will was directed on earth, so shall it be directed after death. Happy the man whose will has been always fixed on God; in other words, who has in his heart the love of God and sanctifying grace; he will see God. Unhappily, many are bent solely on things of the earth, those, for instance, who love the world and are not in the state of grace; they remain separated from God forever. (!) (more on this later, too)

For anyone that has a pang of conscience, chin up! Tell Our Lord you are sorry and want to be with Him forever — like Dismas, turn to Him now, and ask Him, "Remember me, O Lord!"

We don't need to be Uploaded into Computers, but this secret to a Happy Death is EASY!

In order to secure a happy death, we should, in our daily prayer, ask God to grant us a happy death! Also, of our own accord, we must detach ourselves now from earthly goods and pleasures.

Reconcile with God, Put your affairs in Order

I've read this advice in old Catholic texts many times over, "He dies a happy death who is reconciled with God, and has put his worldly affairs in order." It seems like the easy implication to that quip is that we ought often to pray that God may give us the grace to receive the last sacraments before dying. It is also a duty to make a will in good time. If death is like a thief, and if it is the things and attachments that can hold us back, then settling and giving all those things away in a will is to behave like a prudent ship captain who heaves his cargo overboard to avoid shipwreck. That's assuming we can get that done before the unknown moment. It's trickier for sudden death. A sudden death is not a thing to be desired, for we cannot then put into order our spiritual or temporal affairs; hence we pray in the Litanies: "From a sudden and unprovided death deliver us, O Lord." St. Joseph has traditionally came about as the patron of a happy death, and for the grace to avoid a sudden death.

The point of the morbidity is to keep you focused on the importance! "In all thy works remember thy last end, and thou shalt never sin." (Eccles vii 40). St. Ignatius Loyola impresses this thought so firmly in the spiritual exercises that Pope Pius X had an image of himself made and placed in a casket — and when he had an important decision to make, he'd go to the casket, look at himself, and confer with Our Lord as to which choice they'd be happy with when consid-

ered at his death. The secret then, is to remember that we'll all be in that place someday. Whoever thinks seriously of death will take as little pleasure in the things of the world as a criminal with a death sentence will have in a good meal.

Every day's sunset is a reminder from God of death, and sleep is an image of it. It is a lot like Damocles, the sword is right over us! We ought to detach ourselves even now from earthly goods and pleasures! After death our eyes will no longer see, nor our ears hear, nor our tongues speak; and we should prepare for that state by our voluntary restraint now. We should crush the curiosity of the eyes and the ears, our unruly speech and inordinate enjoyment of good, following the counsel of St. Basil : "Let us die that we may live."

The good works which the Church imposes on us, such as prayer, fasting, and almsdeeds, are nothing but a loosening of the heart from earthly ties. Only those who have this detachment shall see God after death: "Blessed are the clean of heart for they shall see God!"

At the end of the Creed, we therefore remind ourselves of all these points: Time flies, our life but a sigh, and here we are ending yet another year. What are you waiting for? When they sing amen for you, do you want to go into the dust caught surprised, or singing alleluia?

So much for Death. We still have three more last things to discuss…

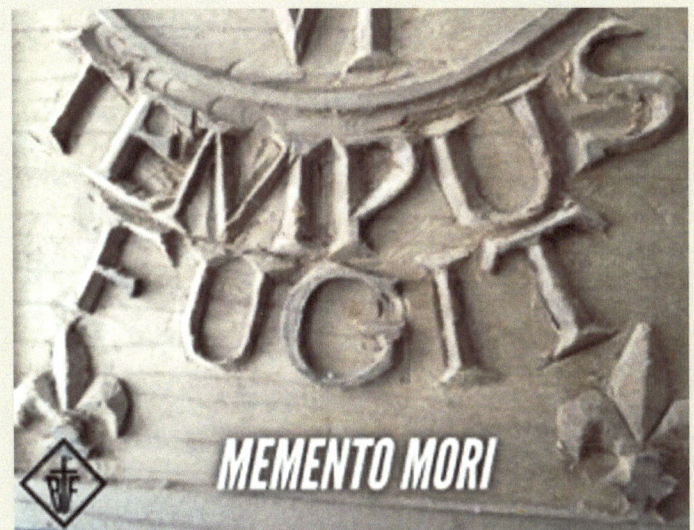

MEMENTO MORI

The Church and Politics

by Stephanie Block

Posted on November 8, 2013

When discussing the problems of faith-based Alinskyian organizing, people frequently will say, "the Church has no business in politics!"

That makes a memorable slogan but it's not true, of course. The truth is complicated.

Blessedly, we have a recent pope who was extremely articulate and capable of expressing complicated truths in clear language and short sentences. In section 47 of *Centesimus Annus*, an encyclical written in 2001 to commemorate the 100th anniversary of *Rerum Novarum*[1], John Paul II wrote that the Church "is not entitled to express preferences for this or that institutional or constitutional solution. Her contribution to the political order is precisely her vision of the dignity of the person."

He's not the first to make that distinction but it's so well said that it bears thinking about.

His point is that the Church has gifts to offer the world, namely the clear expression of foundational truths on which a better earthly world can be built. This earthly world isn't the same thing as "the Kingdom of God," he explains in section 25: "**No political society — which possesses its own autonomy and laws — can ever be confused with the Kingdom of God.**"

Utopians have a tough time accepting that.

So do people who see in the Church a valuable political resource. The Church has "moral capital" that they would like to borrow and invest in whatever scheme is being advanced for the betterment of the world.

John Paul II writes, earlier in the same section, "When people think they possess the secret of a perfect social organization which makes evil impossible, they also think that they can use any means, including violence and deceit, in order to bring that organization into being. Politics then becomes a 'secular religion'."

Which is why it is important to understand when the Church is speaking with authority and when someone — perhaps a high ranking bureaucrat, a religious Sister, or a parish priest — is using the Church to push his or her own preference for this or that institutional or constitutional solution.

Yet, the fellow in the pew (and, through well-managed media, many of the un-pewed) is told that to be a good, compassionate member of the faithful, he must accept and promote whatever the latest action items are presented to him.

Take, for example, the welfare system. Over the years, compassionate Catholics have been given all sorts of directives:

A recent action request from the Office of Justice, Peace and Human Development at the United States Conference of Catholic Bishops (USCCB) was for Catholics to:

"Urge Congress to undertake a full reauthorization of TANF and strengthen the pro-

---

[1] *Rerum Novarum*, published in 1901, was written by Pope Leo XIII to address then-current issues of labor and capital. *Rerum Novarum* denounced socialism and inappropriate State incursion into family life, affirmed workers' rights to form unions and the right of private property, and insisted that a just society must be grounded on Christian principles of charity and subsidiarity.

gram so that it better serves families and individuals in need to help them make a successful transition to work and provide adequately for themselves and their family. Urge Congress to combat the root causes of economic inequality by funding initiatives that reduce poverty and strengthen families, such as marriage education, abstinence programs, responsible fatherhood initiatives especially in low-income communities. Also, it is essential Congress extend low-income tax credits that encourage work. Work with community organizations, local advocates and state officials to assure that states are complying with TANF federal rules and helping families escape poverty."[2]

Whether or not these are good programs isn't the point. The point is whether or not it is appropriate for an official Catholic institution to be pushing them as if they are the Church's position. They aren't.

A citizen with strong moral sensibilities and a compassionate heart might have information about TANF that would make it impossible for him to support precisely because he is convinced it does not strengthen the family, reduce poverty, or combat root causes of income inequity. His reasoning may be every bit as thoughtful — and quite possibly as well-informed — as that proffered by USCCB bureaucrats.

For example, John Paul II recognized and decried a State that turns legitimate and necessary "supplementary intervention" into something excessive. Calling this excess a "Welfare State" or a "Social Assistance State," he writes:

> "By intervening directly and depriving society of its responsibility, the Social Assistance State leads to a loss of human energies and an inordinate increase of public agencies, which are dominated more by bureaucratic ways of thinking than by concern for serving their clients, and which are accompanied by an enormous increase in spending. In fact, it would appear that needs are best understood and satisfied by people who are closest to them and who act as neighbors to those in need. It should be added that certain kinds of demands often call for a response which is not simply material but which is capable of perceiving the deeper human need. One thinks of the condition of refugees, immigrants, the elderly, the sick, and all those in circumstances which call for assistance, such as drug abusers: **all these people can be helped effectively only by those who offer them genuine fraternal support, in addition to the necessary care.**"

[Emphasis added. *Centesimus Annus*, sec 48]

How much "supplementary intervention" is excessive? Is the TANF program an example of excessive intervention? These are issues about which men of good will can disagree and will debate in the public arena. Bring in the "church" to express preferences for this or that institutional or constitutional solution becomes a coercive political move, a way of weighing the debate in favor of a particular outcome by bypassing the debate.

Church teaching is consistent so it's no surprise that the current Pope Francis echoed John Paul's words in a recent interview: "I say that politics is the most important of the civil activities and has its own field of action, which is not that of religion. Political institutions are secular by definition and operate in independent spheres. **All my predecessors have said the same thing, for many years at least, albeit with different accents. I believe that Catholics involved in politics carry the values of their religion within them, but have the mature awareness and expertise to implement them. The Church will never go beyond its task of expressing and disseminating its values, at least as long as I'm here.**"[3] [Emphasis added]

Amen.

2

http://www.usccb.org/issues-and-action/human-life-and-dignity/safety-net-income-support/temporary-assistance-to-needy-families.cfm

3 Interview with Pope Francis by the Founder of Italian Daily "La Repubblica," by *L'Osservatore Romano*, Weekly ed. in English, n. 41, 9 October 2013.

From Under the Rubble...A Bang and a Whimper

by Christopher Manion

Posted on August 19, 2013

Bishop Robert Lynch of St. Petersburg recently complained, "I am convinced that many so called Pro-Life groups are not really pro-life but merely anti-abortion."

Of course, this canard is common among the professional pro-abortion crowd, but it sounds strangely out of tune coming from a Bishop who, in the past, has been supportive of the pro-life movement.

So what's going on?

There's a history here. Since 1960, when candidate John F. Kennedy famously promised in Houston that he would not allow his Catholic faith to interfere with his politics, there has existed among the Catholic hierarchy an influential segment that valued liberal politics more than Church teaching. Various members of this informal cadre advised JFK, welcomed the 1967 rebellion of Catholic universities against Church authority led by Notre Dame, and carefully managed the reputation rehab of Teddy Kennedy after he killed Mary Jo Kopechne at Chappaquiddick two years later.

A key player in the leftward descent of the Catholic Church since the 1960s emerged during the same era. Bishop Joseph Bernardin, who eventually became Cardinal Archbishop of Chicago, was the major influence guiding the Catholic bishops' conference from 1969 until his death in 1996.

At Notre Dame in 2009, Barack Obama repeatedly invoked Cardinal Bernardin, whom he had first met at a community organizing meeting on Chicago's South Side. Bernardin had a "profound influence" on his life, he later told journalists.

Bernardin also had a profound influence on the life of Bishop Lynch. Russell Shaw, longtime spokesman for the USCCB, identifies Lynch as a key player among the "Bernardin Bishops." Lynch joined Bernardin at the headquarters of the bishops' conference in 1972, and served as his alter-ego there for a quarter-century. He became bishop of St. Petersburg the year that Cardinal Bernardin died.

A longtime collaborator of Bernardin is candid: "he wanted to make sure the conference stayed liberal long after he was gone," he tells the Rubble.

With the help of Bishop Lynch, it did. In fact, as Russell Shaw writes, the Bernardin era endured until 2010, when the bishops passed over Bishop Gerald Kicanas, another Bernardin understudy expected to be a shoo-in, and elected instead Timothy Dolan, now Cardinal-Archbishop of New York, as conference president.

Earthquake

The Bernardin years were troubled times for the American Church. As Cardinal Dolan candidly admitted after his election, the bishops hadn't taught the fundamental moral truths of marriage and the family during the Bernardin years – since "the mid- and late-1960s," he said.

Instead, they created a huge bureaucracy that aggressively lobbied Congress, advocating welfare-state programs in the name of "Social Justice," while leaving the Church's moral teaching to gather dust on the shelf.

At the same time, the bishops were taking in a growing amount of federal taxpayer funding for their own charities, which had once been independent, supported by voluntary contributions.

There was a price to pay for this shift in priorities: while the bishops' silence on sexual morality coincided with a startling rise of divorce, contraception, and even abortion among the faithful, it had unhappy consequences within the clergy as well.

The Bernardin era featured dozens of bishops who enabled and covered up for the predominantly homosexual clergy that caused the abuse-and-cover-up scandals. Unfortunately, none of those bishops (save Cardinal Law, and several bishops who were abusers themselves) resigned when the scandals broke. Meanwhile, every priest who was accused of even a remotely indecent act with a child was immediately "disappeared."

"Our credibility on the subject of child abuse is shredded," said Bishop R. Daniel Conlon of Joliet, Ill., a year ago, after he was named to lead the bishops' belated effort to restore that credibility.

The sad truth is, the Bernardin Bishops, having lost it, could not regain it themselves.

That's why the liberal media favorite and Bernardinite Fr. Thomas Reese, S.J., called Dolan's 2010 election "an ecclesial earthquake of monumental proportions." America's younger bishops recognized that they have a gigantic mess on their hands. They had to make up for fifty years of lassitude – and nothing short of an earthquake would do it.

One of the major challenges they confront addresses a cherished legacy of the Bernardin-Lynch years: massive government funding of Catholic entities like the conference, Catholic Relief Services, Catholic Charities U.S.A., and the Catholic Health Association (whose support was essential to the passage for Obamacare).

While Bishop Lynch does complain about the bureaucratic paperwork required by receiving billions of dollars of taxpayer dollars a year, he does not display a similar concern regarding the funding's possible moral consequences.

Cardinal Bernardin recognized, late in life, that tens of millions of dismayed Catholics had left the Church since Vatican II, and millions more who stayed were no longer so generous as they had once been. Perhaps he saw the transformation of the Church's charities into an array of government contractors as a necessary evil: "If we can't trust the faithful to contribute voluntarily, well, we'll ask the government to make it mandatory," the Bernardin bishops seemed to say.

"When the church wants to flaunt its size, build organizations, make departments and become a bit bureaucratic, the church loses its main essence and runs into danger of turning itself into an NGO (Non-Governmental Or-

ganization)," said His Holiness, Pope Francis, last April 24.

Yet the Church's charities, universities, and the conference itself now jostle every year alongside thousands of other NGO's for their share of government funding.

Is the price we paid merely Bishop Lynch's "paperwork"? Or has it been more costly?

The Payoff

Imagine that, for the past fifty years, the Bernardin bishops had followed Canon Law (the law of the Church) and barred from the Eucharist prominent perpetrators of public scandal – specifically, well-known pro-abortion Catholics like Ted Kennedy, Joe Biden, Chris Dodd, Rudy Giuliani, Dick Durbin, John Kerry, Patrick Leahy, Nancy Pelosi, and countless others of both parties.

Would the excommunicated in Congress continue to shell out the dough?

The bishops might actually think that they would. After all, they are nice guys. But that grim bunch of pro-aborts is decidedly not nice. And nothing on Capitol Hill happens without the classic tit-for-tat.

So is the money a payoff for a silent, crucial concession?

Perhaps the bishops don't think so, but the politicians sure do.

Are they right? Consider: why do the bishops lobby for welfare-state programs that harmonize with the liberal agenda, but avoid taking positions that would offend the Left – even though, from Patrick Moynihan in the 1960s to Dr. Patrick Fagan today, researchers have proven many of those welfare programs to be destructive of the family?

And why have conference leaders actually supported legislation that contains hundreds of millions of dollars a year for contraceptives and other "family planning" programs worldwide that are a pivotal priority of this administration?

Meanwhile, the conference is silent on vital issues that collide with the liberal agenda.

Take inflation: it hurts everyone – students, families, the poor, the elderly – all groups which the Church undoubtedly desires to protect.

So why don't we hear moral outrage from the bishops condemning the damage caused by deficit spending and inflationary monetary policies?

And what about domestic "family planning" programs, federal destruction of education, the homosexualization of the military, and the anti-family tax provisions in Obamacare? When have the bishops stormed Capitol Hill in sustained and vocal opposition to those programs the way that they zealously lobby for amnesty, food stamps, and foreign aid?

Perhaps Bishop Lynch complains about "alleged" prolifers because they support the Church's teaching across the board – including Humanae Vitae, which the Bernardin bishops failed to teach. Perhaps they welcome Pope Benedict's critical revision of Church law that requires that "charitable agencies dependent upon [the bishop] do not receive financial support from groups or institutions that pursue ends contrary to Church's teaching." [*Intima Ecclesiae Natura*, Nov. 11, 2012, No.10.3]

Now consider: does the U.S. government, under the most anti-Catholic, anti-life administration in history, "pursue ends contrary to [the] Church's teaching"?

Yes, there is another "earthquake" coming. The marriage of convenience between the bishops and the government, which Bishop Lynch so lovingly nurtured during the Bernardin years, is on the rocks. The real earthquake will come when the funding stops.

The divorce is long overdue. Plead the cause: "Moral cruelty."

In the future, bishops and laity will together have to step up to the plate and revitalize the liberated Church to make it vibrant, independent, charitable, and holy. And then the New Evangelization can proceed with honesty and vigor.

Confusions about Social Justice

by Arthur Hippler

Posted on November 22, 2013

The phrase "social justice" is relatively new, appearing first with frequency in the writing of Pius XI, most notably in *Quadragesimo Anno* (1931). Despite its more frequent use among contemporary Catholics, social justice is now widely confused with its kindred virtues, "commutative justice" and "distributive justice" The failure to distinguish these virtues leads to basic errors about the order of person within society.

When we first think of justice, we tend to think of justice between individuals. This is "commutative" justice and it is shown most clearly in free exchanges. Where individuals exchange goods of equal value, they are according to commutative justice. Fraud and theft are sins against this virtue.

The justice that directs individuals to each other is one kind, but the justice that directs parts to the whole is another. "Social justice" names the virtue that directs individuals toward the common good, as parts to the whole. When one obeys just laws or serves his country in time of crisis, he is not merely ordering himself to another individual but to the community as a whole. However much we may focus on our individual happiness, our perfection lies in seeking the common good beyond our own private good. According to Leo XIII, "no one lives only for his own personal advantage in a community; he lives for the common good as well" [*Graves de Communi*, no.19]. To love the common good as the tyrant does, that is, merely as a means to one's own good, is a sin against social justice.

Besides these two kinds of justice, there is a third: distributive justice. While social justice orders men as parts to the whole, distributive justice orders the society to the citizens as whole to part. When a government honors its veterans, or appoints ministers for its duties, it "distributes" to individuals based on the common good. Distributive justice can be exemplified by its corresponding vice, that is, the "accepting of persons." When a government official is chosen not for his qualification in the service of the common good, but for his wealth or family connections, that is a sin against distributive justice.

Many have fallen into confusing social justice by taking elements from the other kinds of justice and labeling the final product "social justice." From commutative justice, they take the notion of "equality." From distributive justice, they take the notion that the community must distribute to individuals based on their merit. From social justice, they take the notion that the parts are ordered to the whole. Mixing these partial understandings of each virtue together into a kind of ideological soup, the final result is the mistaken belief that "social justice" demands that the society act for individuals in such a way that they are "more equal," as if all inequality were unfair. Social justice would then mean enforced equality.

But all this only distorts the beauty of social justice. Acting for the common good does not demand equality. Indeed, the Popes declare that inequality in possessions and abilities serves the common good, so that those who have more might be joined in justice and charity with those who have less. A society of totally equal and independent individuals is no society at all, only a group of "parts" trying to be "wholes." The virtue of social justice is the ability to act for the common good, even at sacrifice to one's own good. It is not the rearrangement of the social order according to a conflation of "justice" and "equality."

Why Pontius Pilate is in the Apostles Creed, not Judas or the Jews. Gird your loins for the answer.

by John B. Manos

Posted on March 29, 2013

When you follow the Passion this time of year, you hear all the names of various characters: Caiaphas, the high priest; Judas, the wicked disciple; Peter, who pulled out his sword but later denied Our Lord; and the others. One name, however, was put forever in infamy: **Pontius Pilate**. Of all the people and names surrounding the Passion and Crucifixion of Our Lord, why is Pilate singled out in the Apostles Creed by name?

The Infamous Pontius Pilate is mentioned by name in the Apostles Creed

Every time you say a rosary or some other prayer, you say it by name: "…Who was crucified under Pontius Pilate, suffered, died, and was buried."

We don't mention Judas, who is identified from the beginnings of the Church as "the lover of money" (N.B. modern opinions on the matter to the contrary should be discounted in favor of the universal opinion of twenty centuries). Judas does get adequate scorn in many places of the Oriental rites, for instance, the Troparion sung during yesterday's Office and Divine Liturgy:

"When the glorious disciples were enlightened at the washing of the feet, then Judas the ungodly one was stricken and darkened with the love of silver. And unto the lawless judges did he deliver Thee, the righteous Judge. Behold, O lover of money, him that for the sake thereof did hang himself; flee from that insatiable soul that dared such things against the Master."

We also ignore Caiaphas and the Pharisees in general when it comes to the Creed. Worth mention, however, is that the Pharisees get adequate disdain, but not a place in the creed.

But Pilate has name billing. Of blessed memory, Fr. Hardon tells us why: over the centuries, it has been "apostate Christians who have used the State to crucify the martyrs of Christianity."

Stop and re-read that for a moment. Pilate represents the State. Who twists the State to murder Christ? Apostate believers. It's a memorial of Jesus's words to James and John that if they were to follow Him, they must be prepared to drink of His cup. Today is the memorial of that cup.

Fr. Hardon explains this detail of the Passion, with regard to Pilate, this way:

It is not coincidental that Pontius Pilate should be identified in the Apostles Creed. Pilate symbolizes the sufferings and persecution of the Church, which is the Mystical Body of Christ.

The enemies of Christ were the religious leaders of the Jewish people who envied Him. They were, as Jesus more than once told them, hypocrites. They were the chosen priests and teachers of the Chosen People. Yet they misled those whom they were to lead. Their hatred of the Savior was grounded on envy. Thousands followed Jesus to listen to His words. They spent days, even without food, to hear what He had to say. The Scribes and Pharisees had to resort to the most extreme means to have people even pay attention to them. The result was inevitable. This hated Nazarene must die.

There were three main charges which the Jews brought against Jesus. "We have found this man," they claimed "perverting our nation, and forbidding the payment of taxes to Caesar and saying that he is Christ the king" (Luke 23:2).

As we know all these charges were malicious. They were also political in nature. Yet they were enough to sway the cowardly Pilate to condemn Jesus to death.

This has been the history of the Catholic Church ever since. By now millions of faithful followers of Christ have shed their blood for their fidelity to the Savior. Without exception, it has been the Pilates of every age who have been used by Christ's enemies to persecute the Church He founded. The Neros and Attillas, the Huns and Communists have been the agents of the devil in persecuting faithful Christians. But let us be clear. No less than on the first Good Friday, so over the centuries it has been the apostate Christians who have used the State to crucify the martyrs of Christianity.

How can we disagree today? On nearly every front of the Creed, there is an attack, and behind that attack is somebody twisting the State to enforce it.

Memorize the logic of Fr. Hardon above, though: **the apostates use the concerns of the state to force the persecution**. They lie. They manipulate. They even co-opt Bishops, like Judas, to assist them. (how I could go on for hours just on this point alone). The attack doesn't come from outside, but from people close to Jesus. Likewise today, it is often people claiming to be Catholic who are the public face of these manipulations. All of them were motivated by a concern for their own interests, their own feelings, their own futures. Everything, it seems, but the interests of God. So it is today...

At the front of these attacks, though, is Pilate. The fake court trial, the interrogation, and his washing of his hands (as if that did anything) remind us that the state can see Truth, even have a friendly chat with Truth, and still do the wrong thing out of concern to satisfy the apostate manipulators (even the etymology of manipulate explains this, from Latin for "handful").

Let's not be naive, however, and take the cue Mother Church gives us: look what the state did to Our Lord — shall we be any different? The answer is what Father Hardon points out above: no, if we follow Jesus Christ, we won't be any different.

For our part, we should learn from Jesus, Who even under the pain of crucifixion said, "Father forgive them, for they know not what they do." *Even Pilate was the object of that prayer.* As we see Our Lord today, is this part of what He teaches us — that even Pilate deserves forgiveness from us?

For my own part, I think it is, but that is tough...

The Two Standards: Truth Incarnate or The Father of Lies.

by John B. Manos

Posted on May 23, 2013

Recently, I saw a disgusting sight on Kevin O'Brien's blog as people reacted to a post wherein Kevin exhorted people to tell the truth (he gives more examples in his post about this article). The comments are horrid and remind one that no matter how pious and clean the outside, like the Pharisees, it's what one believes and does from the inside that matters. There is a side discussion going on there wherein they are parsing a Chesterton quote on whether one can deceive — the discussion seems to be missing the terms "open mental reservation" versus "closed mental reservations." I'll leave that part of the discussion for another day. Chesterton referred to "Jesuitry" which was a misnomer for an error of the day that attributed Voltaire's justification of lying as if the Jesuits taught it — this has never been true as it was always the case that "The end does not justify the means." Back to the matter of telling the truth:

I've been working on the question of why nobody in the Church talks about telling the truth anymore, especially since I posted the *Theology of the Body (ToB) in One Paragraph* noting that one sure path to chastity is telling the truth (but you'll never hear that from the ToB people — despite the fact that about 10% of JPII's ToB talks were precisely on telling the truth). That's because chastity is a mirror of inside and out — it is to the body what telling the truth is to the mind. It is here — the inconsistency between what is spoken and what is held in the mind where we see it:

Lies are hypocrisy of speech. Telling the truth is a matter of speaking all that one holds in one's mind. Lying is saying something contradictory to the truth held in one's mind. Lying therefore sows error in the minds of others. Error, recall, is synonymous with evil and sin (as Fr. Hardon regularly taught).

Jesus warned the Pharisees of duplicity, clearly stating the problem: "whited sepulchers, which indeed are beautiful on the outside but full of dead mens bones." Liars are by the words they use to project false reality, making themselves different on the outside than they are on the inside. Such duplicity is abhorrent to God, and it's unreal to see anyone attack someone for saying that lying in wrong.

Nevertheless, because nobody talks about the basic duty to tell the truth, I've compiled some motivational catechesis below. It goes without saying that God does not lie — He is truth. Thus, lying is not of God. It's that simple. Yet, since people need to be reminded, here is a mini-catechism on truth.

1. The liar is like the devil and displeasing to God.

He who forfeits the confidence of his fellowmen causes a great deal of harm and is capable of committing all manner of <u>evil</u> [sub sinful or erroneous] deeds.

<u>**The liar resembles the devil, for the devil is a liar and the father thereof**</u> (*John* viii. 44). Remember how the serpent in paradise lied to Eve. Liars are children of the devil, not by nature, but by imitation. The liar is displeasing to God. God is truth itself, and therefore He abhors the liar. Our Lord did

not speak as sharply of any one as of the Pharisees. Why? Because they were hypocrites (*Matt.* xxiii. 27).

Liars and Pharisees Are the only ones not Repented in the Gospels. From every class of sinners He gave an example of one who was saved; e.g., Zacheus among usurers, the good thief among highwaymen, Magdalen and the Samaritan at Jacob's well among profligate women, Saul among persecutors of the Church, but not one single individual among liars and hypocrites did He mention as having sought and found pardon.

Many a time God punished liars severely: witness Ananias and his wife Saphira, who for their falsehood fell dead at St. Peter's feet (*Acts* v.) and Giezi, the servant of Eliseus, who was struck with leprosy for his lies and avarice (*4 Kings* V.). "Lying lips are an abomination to the Lord" (*Prov. xii.* 22).

The liar forfeits the trust of his fellowmen. The shepherd who cried "Wolf" when no wolf was near, found he was not believed when his flock was really attacked; his comrades had been so often deceived that they did not heed his cries. A liar is not trusted when he speaks the truth. He is hated by God and by man.

Liars often do a great deal of harm. The spies who went to view the Promised Land deceived the Israelites by their false report, and alarmed them so that they blasphemed God, wanted to stone the two spies who spoke the truth, and clamored to return to Egypt. See what mischief those men wrought: God declared His intention to destroy the people (*Numb.* xiii.). Jacob deceived his father and obtained his blessing fraudulently; his brother Esau threatened to kill him and Jacob was obliged to take to flight. "He that hath no guard on his speech shall meet with evils" (*Prov.* xiii. 3).

The liar falls into many other sins. "Show me a liar and I will show you a thief." Where you find hypocrisy, you find cheating and all manner of evil practices. A liar cannot possibly be God-fearing. The Holy Spirit will flee from the deceitful (*Wisd.* i. 5). All the piety and devotion of one whose words serve to conceal, not to express his thoughts, is a mere sham; do not associate with such a one, lest he corrupt you

with his ungodly ways. "Lying men are without honor" (*Eccles./Sirach* xx. 28). "The just shall hate a lying word " (*Prov.* xiii. 5).

2. The pernicious habit of lying leads a man into mortal sin and to eternal perdition.

Lying is in itself a venial sin; but it can easily become a mortal sin if it is the means of doing great harm, or causing great scandal. He who indulges the habit of lying runs no small risk of losing his soul, for God withdraws His grace from those who deceive their neighbor. "The mouth that belieth killeth the soul" (*Wisd.* i. 11).

A thief is not so bad as a liar, for the thief can give back what he has stolen, whereas the liar cannot restore his neighbor's good name, of which he has robbed him.

"A thief is better than a man that is always lying; but both of them shall inherit destruction" (*Eccles.* xx. 27). A lie is a foul blot in a man (v. 26).

The soul of the liar is like a counterfeit coin, stamped with the devil's effigy; when at the Last Day, the Judge shall ask: "Whose image is this?" the answer will be "the devil's;" and He will then say: "Render unto the devil the things that are his" (St. Thomas Aquinas). (!)

The Lord will destroy all that speak a lie (*Ps.* v. 7). Liars shall have their portion in the lake burning with fire (*Apoc.* xxi. 8). Our Lord uttered a terrible denunciation of the Pharisees because of their hypocrisy (*Matt,* xxiii. 13). **Lying is consequently forbidden, even if it may be the means of effecting much good.**

St. Augustine says it is just as wrong to tell a lie for your neighbor's advantage as to steal for the good of the poor. Not even to save one's own life or the life of another, is a falsehood justifiable. St. Anthimus, Bishop of Nicomedia, would not allow the soldiers who were sent to arrest him, and who were enjoying his hospitality, to save him by a lie; he preferred to suffer martyrdom. We must not do evil that there may come good (*Rom.* iii. 8). **The end does not justify the means, even if seems like it could.**

Needed:
Catholic Cab Drivers and Bartenders

by John M. DeJak

Posted on June 25, 2013

Some years back–in an interview on EWTN – Francis Cardinal George, Archbishop of Chicago, was addressing some of the pressing needs of the Church. He said–and I paraphrase–"we need Catholic cab drivers and bartenders." It was a comment that elicited a chuckle, but the truth of it was very serious and speaks to the way the Church understands herself and the vocation of the laity. If one stops to think about it, His Eminence is absolutely correct, practical, and– perhaps most important, counter-cultural. Perhaps this simple suggestion of the Cardinal-Archbishop of Chicago could provide a template for a revolution. Come to think of it, it was done once before–but that call was for fishermen.

The first truth implied and enunciated in the Cardinal's comment was the inherent dignity of every human being and his work. It is the opposite view of the reigning cultural elite: What *the world* considers as an important profession or what constitutes success in the eyes of the same *world* is at odds with the teaching of Christ and the Church. Sadly, this basic truth has been forgotten in the years following Vatican II–oftentimes even by bishops and parish priests. In a lecture diagnosing some of the ills that brought us the priestly abuse crisis, Fr. Paul Mankowski, S.J. observed:

> Before the Council every Catholic community could point to families that lived on hourly wages and who were unapologetically pious, in some cases praying a daily family rosary and attending daily Mass. Such families were a major source of religious vocations and provided the Church wi[th] many priests as well. These families were good for the Church, calling forth bishops and priests who were able to speak to their spiritual needs and to work to protect them from social and political harms. Devout working class families characteristically inclined to a somewhat sugary piety, but they also characteristically required manly priests to communicate it to them: that was the culture that gave us the big-shouldered baritone in a lace surplice. Except for newly-arrived immigrants from Mexico, Vietnam and the Philippines, the devout working class family has disappeared in the U.S. and in western Europe.

> The beneficial symbiosis between the clerical culture and the working class has disappeared as well. In most parishes of which I'm aware the priests know how to talk to the professionals and the professionals know how to talk to the priests, but the welders and roofers and sheet-metal workers, if they come to church at all, seem more and more out of the picture. I think this affects the Church in two ways: on the one hand, the Catholic seminary and university culture has been freed of any responsibility to explain itself to the working class, and notions of scriptural inspiration and sexual propriety have become progressively detached from the terms in which they would be comprehensible by ordinary people; on the other hand, few priests if any really depend on working people for their support….

In years past, one could count on Monsignor Such-and-such presiding over the parish finance council meeting that included the lawyer, doctor, and executive before meeting the pipe-fitter and electrician over at the "Nickel Joint" for a few beers before compline. Do our pastors do this today? I suspect such cases are rare.

The second truth implied in the Cardinal's statement is the necessity of the laity to be informed and courageous about their faith. This is none other than the employment of two of the cardinal virtues: prudence and fortitude. *Prudence*–the application of right reason to oneself and his dealing with others and in all situations; and *Fortitude*–a certain firmness of mind and endurance in difficulties (physical or moral). The lay faithful need not have consciously in his head: "Now, I shall employ the virtues of prudence and fortitude." That's just weird. But being virtues, they should be habitual and practiced whether or not the person is conscious of the term! Being well informed of the Faith is a key component. Knowing the articles of the Creed, reflecting on them and the moral teaching of the Church is accessible to and is a necessity for every Catholic. Theological acumen is not necessary, nor is a grasp in the manner of doctors of the Church. It can be very simple. Once apprehended, this knowledge should translate into right thought and action. The person should be confident and firm in these convictions and demonstrate such to his neighbor–even to the point of enduring his neighbor's insults. The important part of this aspect–and that which is apparent by the Cardinal's comment–is that this is the job of every Catholic; not just the CCD teacher, or person who volunteers at the parish. First and foremost this means every Catholic within his own family and sphere of influence. Perhaps the sphere of influence is small; but the touching of another soul is not a small thing–*it has eternal consequences*.

This is where the bartender and the cab driver come in. The sphere of influence of these individuals, in particular, is enormous. Think back to the time you had to grab a cab to get from somewhere to the airport to catch a flight; or perhaps, you were late for a date and needed to meet your sweetheart somewhere and you had to hail a cab. In these situations, did you ever converse with the cabbie? Perhaps he expounded for you–during standstill traffic–his metaphysical ruminations; or his political predictions; or the reason why the cab rates went up 90% in the last year because of new regulations and gas prices. Or maybe you just talked sports. Whatever the issue, the cab driver is a unique individual with a captive audience that may number into the thousands each year. What if a discussion ensued on a great moral issue of the day? His would be an opportunity to defend the poor or the unborn or the Church. Or perhaps, his simple "Merry Christmas" would be a witness to the faith in the face of an ever-rising secularism. He might even bring the car to a screeching halt and dump out a customer for insulting Our Lady.

The same for the bartender. The great American balladeer, Billy Joel, captured the scene beautifully in his hit "Piano Man." The different characters that fill the scene in Joel's imagination seem to capture every class and type of person. They come to the bar for a drink and for different reasons–some looking for companionship, some in pain, some celebrating, some dreaming of something better, some simply thirsty. This is the world of the bartender, it is also the world we live in. All types of people, perhaps thousands each year, visit with the bartender. Consider the influence he might have: a kind word he might offer, taking a stand for the truth during a heated discussion, defending a woman being harassed by a guy, helping a poor weak soul to a cup of coffee, and, yes, kicking someone out of his establishment for something improper or immoral. The Bartender brings joy and also justice to a situation–and as a result, can be a model of Christ in his sphere of influence.

The cab driver and the bartender are solid examples of needed witnesses for Christ and the Church. Most of the time it will not be an explicit articulation of an article of the catechism (though sometimes it might), but it will be a course of action in conformity with and in defense of common sense and a Christian way of life. It may be a simple as the bartender giving the drunk a cup of coffee and hailing a cab, only to have the cabbie ensure that the poor soul gets home unharmed–whether the fare was paid or not. I have long suspected–and it was confirmed by Cardinal George's and Fr. Mankowski's comments: academics giving papers, bloggers or lawyers will not be the most effective ones to change the culture and maintain the faith. It will be moms and dads, welders, roofers, sheet metal workers…and cab drivers and bartenders.

In addition to the aforementioned reasons, perhaps there is also something mystical about cab drivers and bartenders. The one takes you where you want to go; and the other provides you joy, refreshment and contentment. Sounds like an image of the Church to me.

Baseball Cards Without Bubble Gum, 20 Years On

by John M. DeJak

Posted on June 28, 2013

I recall finding out, to my horror, in the early 1990s, that Topps Baseball Card packages were no longer including their trademark brittle piece of gum that had been a mainstay of American boys' youth since the late 1940s and early 1950s. At the time, my card collecting days were over but they were not for my little brother who was around 10. How could he be deprived of the joy and pleasure experienced by so many other boys? This was tradition! How dare the Topps Company take this away? I recall uttering the words: "This is an indicator of the end of a civilization." While my prognostications of cultural decline were that of a high school student, it was curious that forces were coalescing at that time that seemed to indicate that the end was indeed near: the Clinton Presidency, MTV Spring Break, and hairspray-laced scalps of girls that doubled as antennae for homes that did not have cable-television. That said, upon reflection 20 years later, the exclusion of bubble gum from baseball card packages serves as a metaphor for our cultural decline and a subtle war against—and certain disregard for—the most valuable resource of any society: children.

Historically speaking—as I understand—baseball cards were originally called "bubble gum cards." I first heard the term as it was uttered by Lucy in her dismissal of Beethoven's prestige and fame to a horrified Schroeder in "A Charlie Brown Christmas." Apparently, the cards were actually inserted to bolster falling bubble gum sales in the late forties and early fifties. (Thus, I am not naive to any purely altruistic motives of bubble gum companies.) In any event, the relationship between baseball cards and gum was inseparable from the beginning. Indeed, it was the same with the game. Along with tobacco, sunflower seeds, hot dogs and cracker jacks, bubble gum and baseball go together like bacon and eggs or beer and pretzels. But suddenly, in the early 90s, (business-)man put this asunder.

Boys in the early years of this divorce knew intimately the disappointment of what they were missing. Indeed, I imagine there were protests from several quarters at the time, but over the years it became an accepted reality. Memories of what had once been—the joy, the excitement, the childhood tradition–had faded with time. Young boys today have no concept of that grand tradition of baseball card collecting in the same way that boys who grew up in the 1950s through the 1980s. So why the sundering of bubble gum from baseball cards? I don't know the definitive answer, but I will make bold to speculate. Given our cultural mores, perhaps my conclusions will bear out.

In the early 1990s, I suspect that the reason that the manufacturers stopped including bubble gum was simply the profit motive. The folks in the board room probably had the discussion—as all businesses do—of how to cut costs and make more profit. I'm sure that there were probably studies done and perhaps investigations undertaken to isolate where profit derived from. We all know the result, get rid of the gum. The paradox—at least in the case of Topps—is that the corporation was named the The Topps Chewing Gum Company, Inc., yet there was no chewing gum in one of their most popular products. This raises several questions of a philosophical nature: (1) What is the purpose of a business or company? (2)

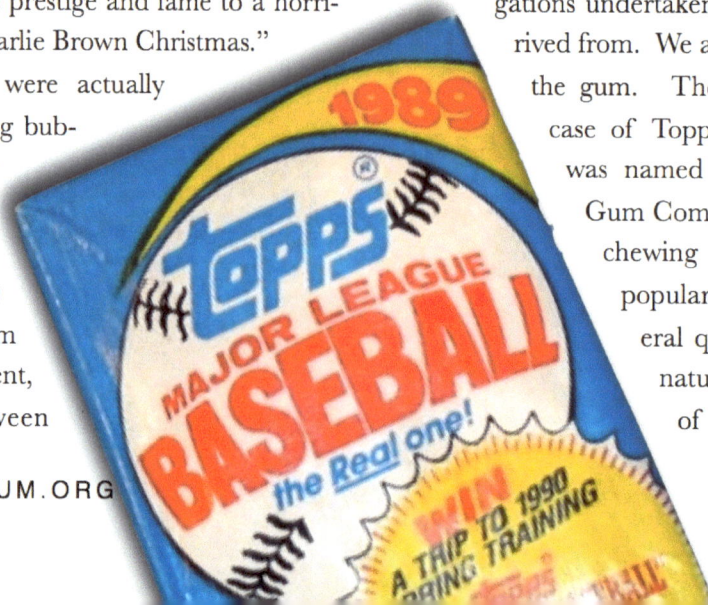

Is it founded to produce a product or provide a service or is it simply an arrangement to get profit? (3) If the latter part of #2, does it owe any responsibilities to the public at large or the common good and how is it kept accountable? (4) When is it acceptable to change the very nature of a company and how does one do it?

Another reason is the shifting focus of the target audience from children to adults. In the early 1990s, one sees a shift away from producing bubble gum and baseball cards as primarily for the kids, and a turn to the collectors' market. In other words, the business had subtly taken a new approach—that of marketing towards adults. The sports collector industry is big business and the bubble gum-baseball card companies saw this as a way to increase their profit. Thus, by eliminating the costs associated with inclusion of gum and the possible imperfections that the sugary treat might place upon the cards, the manufacturer focused on the pristine nature of the cards and developing other "lines" of cards that would serve the collector market.

Traditionally it seems, boys would collect the cards—buying individual packs and hoping to get the players from their hometown teams. They would trade with their friends, learn the stats of their favorite players, and use the cards of the no-name rookies as an "improvised motor" for their bikes, having affixed the card to the frame of the bike and letting the spokes hit them simulating the sound of a Harley. Collecting cards was for fun—part of the excitement that every new spring brought in anticipation of the upcoming season. Now, collecting is judged by how much a card is worth in monetary terms. The focus—even for the kids today—is not fun, but rather how much a card is worth. There is also no longer the excitement and anticipation of opening individual packs to see what players were obtained; today, in most stores, the full set is on display and for sale. The immediate gratification of obtaining the whole set is sated and there is no self-limitation or excited antici-pation of obtaining your favorite players. The virtues of patience and temperance seem to take a back seat.

Some may say that I am making too much of baseball cards and bubble gum. Perhaps I am, but I think it is a metaphor for the cultural collapse that we see around us. To a startling degree, the world is more and more polytheistic. Two gods vie for our worship, Mammon and Moloch, (or many more if one considers the fascination with self-worship today) and the high priests of such are big business but-tressed by big government with the advertising de-partment of the media. The insatiable desire for gold destroys the virtues of temperance (i.e., virtuous self-limitation), generosity and patience, and cares not for its ripple effects on people and families—especially children. Unbridled license with regard to economic matters provides cover for unbridled license in other areas. We have seen how *Roe v. Wade* has enshrined in our law that the unborn child is not a person. Func-tionally, the dominant economic atmosphere and po-litical philosophy have similarly enshrined that the born child is not a person either. (Witness this week's Supreme Court decision.) Very little cognizance is taken, in the economic or political sphere, of chil-dren—except where they may be at the service of adults. Thus, everything in our culture—entertain-ment, economic, political—is geared towards adults. Paradoxically, it is the adults who are acting like spoiled children—unpracticed in virtue, demanding immediate gratification and, in many cases, the satis-faction of their greed and libidinous desires. This is not what Our Lord meant when He said that one must become like a little child if he wishes to enter the kingdom of heaven. Indeed, as He will come again, I predict that Mammon's and Moloch's (and the al-mighty Self's) bubbles are about to burst.

What Really Killed the Catholic Church in America

by John B. Manos

Posted on May 2, 2013

Appearing on a heavily trafficked blog today is an article by Fr. Dwight Longenecker titled What's Killing American Catholicism. In it, Father Longenecker says two things worthy of note:

1. Ethnic Parishes destroyed America (!). Literally, he says "The first problem is cultural Catholicism". I am flabbergasted and nearly speechless at the ignorance of this statement. His conclusions thereto are even more fantasy. He somehow conflated ethnic tradition with mainstream American Catholic Church lunacy: "This is the core problem with Cultural Catholicism: by its very nature it goes with the flow."

2. Father is looking at ethnic traditions *from the outside*. He doesn't understand it, evidenced by this quote: "I was brought up as an Evangelical fundamentalist." While Father goes on to explain that he understands traditions. I don't find any of his explanations of Mennonite and other Anabaptist faiths to be compelling, however. Those are, after all, traditions that sought to rid themselves of humanity in favor of an insular "circle the wagons" in a safe community.

Father concludes with a fancy sounding label he created: "The answer to Cultural Catholicism, therefore, is what I call Comprehensive Catholicism—a Catholicism that embraces all things for their essential worth." I have to laugh at it. He wants to make something up whole cloth from scratch.

I've got news for him: people did that for the last twenty centuries and it's called "tradition." G.K. Chesterton calls tradition "the democracy of the dead." People who lived through depressions, gnosticism, heresy, secular governments, martyrdom, aggressive cults and sects, as well as faithless priests and bishops figured out the "Best practices" and the "comprehensive solutions." We call it ethnic traditions.

Father is recounting his casual experience with the children of ethnic tradition, but he leaves something out: those people have been assaulted by AmChurch. Yes, Father needs to account for the errors that are forced from within the AmChurch — they infect and destroy the cultureless, and this infection has been so festered that even ethnic traditions have been affected. What are the festering errors? It's not ethnicity. Father seems to prefer the culture-less, whitewashed Church, like this one:

There is nothing from tradition or ethnicity invading that "worship space!" It truly is a vacuum! You can bring whatever you want to that space and <u>nothing</u> in there will confront you with opposing ideas. That's the AmChurch!

Over the years, I have heard Fr. Hardon give many explanations of the problems in the Church. Never did Fr. Hardon, or any other priest that I recall, complain that ethnic tradition was killing the Church. Rather, I've heard the following, and this is not an exhaustive list by any means:

1. **Lack of clear teaching on basic Catholic faith. Error is not promptly crushed or**

corrected by the Bishops – that's their purpose, yet we've seen:

- Silence on the erroneous assertion that God is not a person, but a genderless "thing;"

- Silence on the assertions that the miracles in the Gospel are mere stories or myths;

- Silence on the errors propagated by liberation theologians (social activism, Marxism, *etal.*);

- Silence on *Humanae Vitae* – despite what Fr. Longenecker says, implying that people think contraception is OK is caused by ethnic traditions — the real cause is that his confreres and bishops have ignored the teaching for over forty years. It starts, as Fr. Hardon would say, with contraception (see Fr. Sauppe's take [earlier in this booklet], too);

- Silence on divorce and excessive grants of annulments leading the faithful to a diminished understanding of the sacrament of matrimony; and,

- Silence on the morality of telling the truth (seriously, when is the last time you heard this basic concept preached?).

2. Actual error taught to the faithful:

- Fr. Hardon recounted the story that an Archdiocese refused to give him an imprimatur on a small booklet about the Blessed Sacrament unless Father would remove the words "real presence" before the reference to Jesus;

- I can recall being told by numerous priests (and one archbishop) that the Blessed Sacrament was a symbol, never referencing that a physical real Person is there;

- I can recall being told by priests in AmChurch parishes that confession is arcane, and that God could hear your confession anywhere;

- That sin is "institutional" and "social" without ever referencing actual sin, that is, error by the person; and,

- That hell is imaginary and implying that everyone goes to Heaven, no matter their choices.

3. Liturgical Abuses:

- Liturgical Dance;

- The removal of Gregorian Chant and traditions of the Roman Rite;

- the regular use of so-called "eucharistic ministers" which are properly called "extraordinary ministers" (because they are only supposed to be used in extraordinary circumstances);

- the tinkering with the english language, which is not resolved (I think the ICEL psalms are terrible);

- the destruction of devotions, statues, things of beauty;

- the construction of empty churches that have no statues, no painting;

- removal of kneelers;

- bowing instead of genuflecting;

- removal of gestures of faith during the liturgy; and,

- the insertion of inane music to the Mass (guitars, hippy music, and other experiments of things devoid of ethnic tradition).

This list can easily be expanded. Any of these are fatal to the Church. None of these have anything to do with ethnic parishes but with the American hierarchy and the parishes therein.

Ethnic Traditions are Part of Genuine "Comprehensive Catholicism"

The traditions I learned of Polish customs surrounding the Church are literally "Comprehensive Catholicism." Good lay people strong with traditions have been the ones that have preserved the true faith — despite the onslaught of the AmChurch. Frankly, a lot of what I read from the Bellarmine Forum (even though it was called *Wanderer Forum Foundation* back then) over the years helped immensely. It is, literally, lay people coming from ethnic traditions that could see the destruction of the Church occurring around them and said "enough!" Documents and newsletters of the Forum weren't welcome in AmChurch parishes. I can remember seeing them traded like contraband among little old ladies who still had prayer sodalities at their houses (because the parish priest refused to give them space at the parish church) and among regular blue-collar guys who talked briefly between wrangling their children.

For Fr. Longenecker to lay blame on someone other than the crazy experiments carried out in the "spirit of Vatican II" is not very realistic. Whatever else I can say about ethnic Catholicism is that it is real: it has to be. Let's be real about what killed the Church in America: ignorant, empty-headed, incessant tinkering with the faith.

I find it funny that among the various ethnic parishes I've been at, the old folks all complain of the same thing: assimilation by the culture-less American Church destroying their children.   For them, the **AmChurch has been a gateway drug to nondenominational worship by their kids.** That is, among other things, what the ethnically cleansed parishes of the AmChurch were: nondenominational, noncharactered, nonsacramental, nontraditional, bland, whitewashed, and non-Catholic.

Little Vinny doesn't believe in the sacraments anymore not because he went to St. Anthony's Grotto Parish with quarterly ravioli dinners and a giant festival to St. Anthony every year.   Little Vinny doesn't believe because he experienced AmChurch which has no ravioli, no ties to history, no statues, no sacraments, and no faith. It's really that easy.

The problem in the Catholic Church today is that it has made a generation and a half of little Vinnys, little Seans, little Margaritas, little Sashas, and given them a false belief that what AmChurch taught them is really the Church.   One of the only things that might possibly provoke these people to wake up and realize that AmChurch was wrong is the niggle of ethnic traditions. Why? because it carries with it the democracy of all those people who built it with features of Catholic faith. Such traditions are an integral part of anything we might call "comprehensive Catholicism."

THE
WEAPON
OF PEACE

Fr. Hardon: Three reasons why the devil is so strong today.

by John B. Manos

Posted on February 17, 2014 (Bonus)

Speaking in 1992, Father Hardon was asked this question "Minding the rise of heresy and the participation of even priests and religious in the acceptance of homosexuality, the changes in the Mass, and the so-called modern morality, why is the Devil so apparently strong today?"

Answered Father Hardon:

"For three reasons. And the Devil *is* extraordinarily strong and successful today:"

Penalty.

"First, as penalty for sins committed … in other words… we believe in the solidarity in virtue and solidarity in sin. We believe that the present generation can be suffering for the sins of the past generation."

Judases in the Church. (!)

"Second reason, God is allowing the Devil to be so successful because those who should be guiding the Church in sound morality are not doing so! In other words, the Catholic Church depends, absolutely depends on the authority established by Christ when he ordained the apostles at the Last Supper. And, therefore, the Devil is so successful because the Devil, remember, he succeeded with one apostle, Judas. Judas was possessed by the Devil. *Do you hear me?* And he allowed himself to be possessed by the Devil to betray Christ. There are Judases in the Catholic Church today. And I am quoting Pope Paul VI. He knew exactly what he was saying."

That more grace abound.

"Third reason, and consolingly, God allows such massive evil in today's world being perpetrated by the Devil because God, in his Infinite Providence, plans to give extraordinary blessings on the generation before

us. the century to come. In other words, in the spirit of St. Paul, where sin has more abounded … get the "more" … the grace will … get the future tense … the grace will even more abound. The 21st century, says the Holy Father, will be the holiest and most Catholic century of the Church's history. But we've got to do our part. And I know I am talking to the right audience."

It's not a light accusation when Fr. Hardon says that someone was possessed – it a a technical and theological conclusion. After all, the Gospels record that at the last supper, Satan entered Judas. This was not hyperbole or metaphor.

What is more striking is the quote from Paul VI. I had not heard that before, or if I had, I didn't pay attention to it.

The context missing in this answer is that earlier in the talk, Fr. Hardon was speaking on the necessity of Catholics to earn (merit) grace by suffering their faith. He spoke on pain, real pain, as in the cross, being the method of earning that grace.

When we consider that Arius was a bishop, or Nestorius for that matter, it shouldn't be a surprise that there'd be Judas in the Church, should it? Dante's *Inferno* places many in hell, but people tend to write him off as merely politically motivated. He pictured Judas at the lowest level of hell with satan himself — the worst punishment being saved for treacherers, right next to the frauds.

Is it shocking, though, because Pope Paul VI said there are more than one? What else could explain the open and clear dissent that various bishops had from *Humanae Vitae*?

Or, even worse, in the failure of these Judases Paul VI mentions to lead the Church with sound

moral authority, and with clear teaching on the sacraments, such as the Real Presence of Jesus in the Blessed Sacrament or the indissolubility of Holy Matrimony? (I mentioned this failure in *What Killed the Catholic Church in America...* but I restrained myself from calling them Judases on my own estimation. Now I have authoritative statements of the same.)

And look at reason number 3! Think of the graces you can merit, however, in this time, by merely growing your faith and standing with the true faith! We are today like St. John Chrysostom, surrounded by error! Just keeping the basic faith of the Church is painful today! Others have left through schism, such as people I've known in my life who are now sedevacantists or in schismatic groups. Or other friends, unhappy in the Church teaching on contraception or marriage, have left for a nondenominational "feel good" church. Or worse, some that are neopagans, and worship their own will. They claim that the Church is somewhere else. Too bad... there was grace to be earned staying with Jesus in His Church. Maybe they will come to their senses yet by some of the graces we can earn enduring their taunts and jeers.

Imagine if the Apostles had done that and left merely because Judas showed up. St. Peter had it right: to whom would they go? No, sticking it out, hanging in there all the way until Easter is what God expects of us.

Easter always comes.

Are you in the Battle or not?

EPILOGUE

For 48 years, the Bellarmine Forum has been your source for the defense of the faith, but now you've read why. Our topics and concerns aren't always the popular, or even the things that the world notices, but they are a reliable and provocative view of the Church. For instance, our analysis of Pope Francis from the very first full day of his being pope has been with a forgotten lens: the rules of life given by St. Ignatius Loyola in his Spiritual Exercises. While the popular commentary of Catholic topics may have forgotten or never known these things, we didn't forget, and time has shown that we had a firm grasp on understanding this Pope from day 1. Many are still struggling to understand his perspective yet today. That's because they haven't read what we had to say.

You've seen it in these pages: thoughts, concepts, and traditions of the Church that are useful and part of the Church are alive and well here. We hope this clear thinking, and plain speech, will continue to be a sign that we love Mother Church and want to proclaim Her glory, from Our Lord!

The Bellarmine Forum will continue to strive to be this reliable voice in the din of our day, and we are glad you are part of us. As we approach 50 years, we are proud of the way we've used the graces God has bestowed on us, and we hope that He continues to give us the means we need to continue and speak well on His Church.

Pray with us, and for us!

Prayer for Generosity

St. Ignatius of Loyola

Eternal Word, only begotten Son of God,
Teach me true generosity.
Teach me to serve you as you deserve.
To give without counting the cost,
To fight heedless of wounds,
To labor without seeking rest,
To sacrifice myself without thought of any reward
Save the knowledge that I have done your will.
Amen.

PHOTO CREDITS

White House photo by Eric Draper. Pope Benedict XVI acknowledges being sung happy birthday by the thousands of guests Wednesday, April 16, 2008, at his welcoming ceremony on the South Lawn of the White House. Public Domain. source: http://commons.wikimedia.org/wiki/File:Bush_and_Benedictus_81st_birthday_2008.jpg

Used under GNU license located at http://commons.wikimedia.org/wiki/File:Benedykt_XVI_i_Lech_Kaczyński_modlitwa.jpg from Polish Government archives.

From left to right are Bishop Wiktor Skworc, Cardinal Joseph Ratzinger and Cardinal Franciszek Macharski on May 10, 2003, during the celebration of the 750th anniversary of the canonization of Saint Stanislaus in Szczepanów, Poland. Picture taken by Marian Lambert and released under CC-BY license by Szamil. http://commons.wikimedia.org/wiki/File:Ratzinger_Szczepanow_2003_5_modified.jpg

Permission to use under CC-SA-BA-3.0 by Tenan. http://commons.wikimedia.org/wiki/File:Papa_Francisco_recién_elegido.jpg

Agência Brasil, a public Brazilian news agency, provides this under CC-A 3 Brazil license. http://commons.wikimedia.org/wiki/File:Pope_Francis_at_Vargihna.jpg

Permission and license by CCA-SA-3 by FCzarnowski. http://commons.wikimedia.org/wiki/File:Francis_Inauguration_fc10.jpg

Casa Rosada grants license by CC-SA 2 http://commons.wikimedia.org/wiki/File:Cristina_Fernandez_de_Kirchner_with_Franciscus_19032013_2.jpg

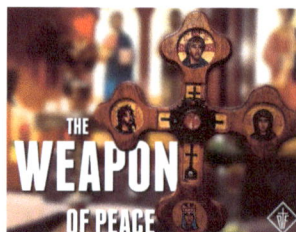

Agência Brasil, a public Brazilian news agency, provides these under CC-A 3 Brazil license.

Allison McKellar, CC-A-2 http://commons.wikimedia.org/wiki/File:El_Salvador_killed_more_than_75.000.jpg

© John B. Manos. Used with permission.

cover photo component by Matthias Kabel http://commons.wikimedia.org/wiki/File:Fountain_of_Carlo_Fontana_on_Piazza_San_Pietro_at_night.jpg

cover photo component by El Caballero http://commons.wikimedia.org/wiki/File:Blesk.jpg

www.ingramcontent.com/pod-product-compliance
Lightning Source LLC
LaVergne TN
LVHW072107070426
835509LV00002B/51